AF559990

MATERIALS MANAGEMENT

MATERIALS MANAGEMENT

By

Dr. M. Karthikeyan
Assistant Professor
Department of Cooperatives
Faculty of Business & Economics
Hawassa University
Hawassa
Email: mkeya2003@gmail.com
mkeya2003@yahoo.com

&

Prof. S.Nakkiran
Professor
Department of Cooperatives
Institute of Cooperatives & Development Studies
Ambo University
Ambo, Ethiopia
E-mail: doctorsnakkiran@gmail.com

DISCOVERY PUBLISHING HOUSE PVT. LTD.
NEW DELHI-110 002

Published by:
Tilak Wasan

DISCOVERY PUBLISHING HOUSE PVT. LTD.
4383/4A, Ansari Road, Darya Ganj
New Delhi-110 002 (India)
Phone : +91-11-23279245, 43596064-65
Fax : +91-11-23253475
E-mail : parul.wasan@gmail.com
discoverypublishinghouse@gmail.com
web : www.discoverypublishinggroup.com

First Edition: **2012**
ISBN: 978-93-5056-049-5

Materials Management

Printed at:
Shree Balaji Art Press
Delhi

Preface

Dear Learners! It is our pleasure to introduce the textbook ***Materials Management*** to you. This book is designed in a detailed manner so as to help you to understand the application of various concepts on materials management. This book covers the concepts on materials management, purchasing, materials handling and maintenance, value analysis, vendor rating, inventory management and transportation.

This work is based on our experience as teachers, trainers and researchers in the field of cooperatives. The present work is based on Under Graduate programme and outcome of our teaching and research experience, articles published in reputed journals, and discussions with cooperative officials. This book will be very much useful to the student of under graduate, and also to professionals involved in materials department, and the trainers who are working in various training establishments. We have drawn the inputs from various materials; papers, journals, books and we have consulted several of our friends, colleagues and field experts. We are ever grateful and thankful to them for their immense support and healthy criticism. We hope that the readers of this book will get knowledge on materials management. Any useful comments, suggestions to improve the present version are welcome and solicited from the readers. We are thankful and grateful to Parul Wasan, Discovery Publishing House Pvt. Ltd., New Delhi for publishing this book neatly under his renowned label for the knowledge community.

M. KARTHIKEYAN

S. NAKKIRAN

Contents

Functions and Benefits of Materials Management

Definition of Materials Management

Ammer defines materials management as "the process by which an organization is supplied with goods and services that it needs to achieve its objectives. The materials management begins with the supplier and ends when the material is consumed or incorporated into some other product. The executives who engage in materials management are concerned with three basic activities—buying, storage of materials, and movement".

International Federation of Materials Management - Materials management is a total concept involving an organizational structure unifying into a single responsibility, the systematic flow and control of material from identification of the need through customer delivery.

Men, money, machines and materials are the keys to development. Generally organizations give poor importance to materials management and resulting in inefficiency. Materials management improves the productivity of an organization. Improper management of materials may saddle the organization and block the precious capital which can be used productively for some other purpose or break down the production process by poor supply of raw materials. On the other hand any significant contribution made by materials manager in reducing the cost of materials would increase the profit of the organization.

Materials management can be defined as the process of planning, sourcing, purchasing, storing, and controlling the flow of materials in an optimum manner so as to facilitate the production process.

Functions of Materials Management

Based on the above definition, the scope of materials management is vast. However, broadly the functions of materials management include the following:

1. Planning

Planning is a process whereby the materials management works to optimize the conflicting objectives of having a minimum investment in inventory with that of always having material on hand to meet the needs of manufacturing departments within the organization. It includes the following functions:

- Determination of materials requirements
- Production scheduling according to the requirement, keeping in view the various constraints
- Planning of inventories—determination of stock levels, recorder timings and quantities etc.
- Coordinating various activities of material management to improve efficiency (reduce paper work, eliminate duplication etc)
- Liaison with other functions of management
- Classification and codification of materials

2. Procurements

Procurement starts with the sourcing the viable source of purchase and ends with the maintaining good relationship with the supplier. Other activities connected with the procurement are:

- *Market research for materials*—development of most suitable source, purchasing research

- Value Analysis—Substitute development
- Negotiations, pricing and placing of orders
- Expediting and follow-up of purchase orders
- Contracting of labour, transport and other services (for handling of materials)
- Insurance of materials
- Disposal of surplus, obsolete and scrap material

3. Receiving and Storage

Storage manages the materials against the damage, theft, fire, etc. Scientific storage ensures the safety, cost reduction and easy flow of goods. The activities involved in this function are:

- Receipt of materials, unpacking, entering into books etc.
- Inspection of materials, approval (or rejection) storage of approved materials (or return of rejected materials)
- Handling and maintaining physical inventories periodic stock verification (reconciliation with book balances)
- Maintaining stock records and Bin cards (or kaidex) etc.
- Indenting of stock items
- Physical inventory control
- Packing of final product
- Issue of materials

4. Movement and Transportation

Transportation plays significant role in the management of materials. Availability materials in right quantity and in right time rest with this function. This function includes the following activities:

- Transportation of materials, minimizing transportation costs
- Clearing of various shipments, incoming as well as outgoing at various points (Excise, octroi, customs etc.)

- Claims for losses and damages
- Dispatching of finished goods

Types of Materials Required by an Industry

Any manufacturing industry must use the following materials:

- *Raw Material:* The materials used are in the natural or original state without having undergone any processing. Cooperatives like sugar cooperatives use sugarcane as raw material.
- *Purchased Parts:* These are the finished products of other industries engaged in the manufacture of items like nuts, screws, bolts, etc. In other words, what is finished product for one industry is just another material required for the other industry.
- *Semi-processed Materials:* the manufacturing unit obtains these either by sub-contracting or by direct buying from another unit. Such semi-processed items may be required because of lack of capacity in its own plant or due to lack of special knowledge to produce that material.
- *Material Supplies:* These items are these which are used in the manufacturing process but do not themselves enter into the final product like chemicals, dies, files, beltings, etc.
- *Equipment:* These are not materials in the ordinary sense of the term. They are rather assets like lathes, drills, replacement items for assets. Nevertheless, they have to be bought and, therefore, can be classified as purchases.

Importance of Materials Management

The importance of materials management can be realized from the benefits gained from a materials management organization. Fearon gives the following sixteen benefits:

1. Elimination of buck passing

Defining and centralizing the authority and responsibility for all the materials functions with one key individual provide a central point of control for the total flow materials in the system. When using departments have problems regarding their material requirements, they can look to one central point within the organization for answers and action. No longer will the material user whose requirements have not been adequately satisfied need to 'chase down' the 'bottleneck' in the material flow, and often become very frustrated when he find that the 'difficulty' preventing the prompt satisfaction of his requirements always seems to be 'someone else's responsibility'.

2. Better inter-departmental cooperation

This is accomplished both between the materials management function and major departments within the total organization and also with the various sub-functions that make up the materials management organization. Using departments find that they receive better more efficient service from the materials organization. This creates an atmosphere conductive to solving material user-supplier problems with a sense of mutual trust and co-operation.

3. Lower prices for materials and equipment used

Wise buying requires accurate information promptly supplied regarding materials needs. This enables purchasing to take advantage of things such as quantity buying use of various types of blanket orders and other types of contract buying, arrangements and buying in anticipation of market changes. When all materials functions, including materials planning and control and inventory control are joined together organizationally, communication regarding material requirements is greatly expedited.

4. Faster inventory turnover

Due to the greater speed, accuracy and completeness of communication regarding material requirements and usage rates, it is often possible to reduce the total investment in inventory. With resultant savings in inventory costs, indeed, some firms found that centralization of materials functions resulted in a 20-40 per cent reduction in size of material stocks. In addition better more responsive inventory purchasing decisions have enabled some firms to reduce the number of inventory stock-outs. while at the same time reducing inventory.

5. Continuity of supply

Disruptions in operations are extremely costly to an organization. Yet disruptions do occur, often because of breakdowns in communications between various materials functions or lack of cooperation between functions. Materials management fosters the needed co-operation, communication and coordination, which help prevent such disruptions.

6. Reduced material lead time

With long communication channels a substantial amount of time may elapse between the dates a potential material user recognizes his need and the time that material is received by the company. If this information must be transmitted to materials planning and control, then to inventory control and finally to purchasing and if these three functions are not in close organizational proximity several days may elapse before the purchase order even goes to a vendor. Additionally, there is a chance that because of the organizational distance between these functions, urgency in material needs may be misunderstood. The net result may be that purchasing is slow to react to needs, and thus procurement lead times are longer than necessary. Under materials management, this reaction time should be less, and material lead times shortened.

7. Reduced transportation costs

Although even under the materials management type organization certain purchases may be shipped by premium-cost transportation methods to meet emergency material requirements, the overall materials-traffic bill should be less. Under integrated materials management, there will be better, more thorough planning of material needs, which will enable the scheduling of incoming materials traffic to take advantage of minimum-cost shipping methods.

8. Less duplication of effort

When the materials system is set up as an integrated whole, overlap of record keeping and clerical work can be reduced. Duplicate records are often kept to avoid losing time in going to another point in the organization to get information, and because of distrust in records maintained in other parts of the organization. Since all materials functions are in constant, close contact under materials management, duplicate records need not be maintained. One set of records, easily accessible to all functions requiring the information will suffice. Also, one report can often take the place of several reports and at a savings in clerical effort.

9. Reduced personnel

With the reduced duplication of effect that comes about through the materials management concept, it is often possible to reduce the total number of people throughout the organization who are performing materials functions and at the same time to raise the level of efficiency with which the organization's materials needs are satisfied.

10. Better morale

People normally work better as part of a team. For example, if the individual(s) performing the receiving function is placed under the Materials Manager he becomes part of an important team. The materials management concept joins together many people whose work overlaps. With such overlapping of duties, these individuals often fight to assert their authority and quite agile at dodging responsibility. However, when these individuals are united, with clearly defined objectives and duties they will co-operate. Materials management affords people an increased status in the organization and this will be reflected in increased morale.

11. Development of personnel

When an individual is part of only his own functional department, such as purchasing, his personal development and promotional possibilities are limited. But as a member of the materials management organization, the individual's opportunity to gain familiarity with the broader aspects of materials is much enhanced. His opportunity for personal growth and development is increased.

12. Reduced materials obsolescence

The greater control exercised over materials in inventory, and the more accurate balancing of materials acquisitions with materials usage, minimize the possibility of losses through materials obsolescence. In addition, the close tie-in-between scrap and surplus disposal and the other materials functions provides for the prompt identification of obsolete items and their efficient disposal.

13. Improved vendor relations

The close co-ordination which materials management provides between purchasing and other materials functions gives purchasing the information that is vital to planning the procurement requirements and in establishing workable purchasing-vendor arrangement. The more fully and accurately purchasing can communicate it needs to vendor the more satisfactory will be the relationship between purchasing and vendors. Through this close coordination, purchasing can improve vendor relation by establishing delivery schedule and the on basis of complete and up to the minute knowledge of inventory levels and usage requirements and by eliminating peak-and-value delivery requirements frequent rescheduling of delivery time and the placement of short lead time others.

14. Better records and information

The centralization all information on materials activities in one organizational location enable the preparation of more comprehensive and accurate records the information necessary to gain a total perspective on specific materials problems is readily available. In addition it is possible for materials manager to acquire easily a total information needed to plan and the monitor the entire materials flow systems.

15. Better control of quality

The quality control functions of the materials management organization permits consistent control of, those items received in the organization. Due to the coordination and communication between the quality control and the other materials people quality standards will be more consistently applied. Variation from quality standard can be promptly relayed to other materials departments needing this information enabling them to react quickly.

16. Facilitation of data processing systems

The centralization all materials information makes possible the design and implementation of fast efficient systems for gathering, summarizing and analyzing data which can be used to facilitate the smooth flow of materials. Data processing system cannot be designed efficiently on a piecemeal basis. The materials management concept makes the utilization of such advanced data processing systems economically faceable and practical.

Importance of Materials Management in Cooperatives

- Cooperatives are working under competitive circumstances. Hence they have to be efficient in procuring and handling materials survive in the competition.
- Efficient materials management practice alone can ensure effectiveness of the operations of cooperatives.
- Earning of surplus (profit) depends on, among other factors, efficient materials management practices.
- Over stocking of materials resulting in unnecessary locking of capital is avoided by prudent materials management practices cooperatives.

- Wastages of raw materials and pilferages could be avoided by better material management in cooperatives.
- Ultimately, the cost of production can be brought down by the cooperatives. This benefit can be transferred to the members.

Challenges for Cooperatives in Materials Management

- During several times, cooperatives suffer from shortage of raw materials. This is due to wrong location of the factories.
- Productivity of cooperative is low compared to private sector. Attention should be paid to this by units like cooperative sugar factories.
- The personnel are not well trained in the cooperative sector. They are yet to be trained in modern materials management techniques.
- Many processing cooperatives like sugar cooperative lack sufficient working capital. The result is that they are not paying the members the amount due to then, in time.
- Value analysis technique should be observed efficiently by the cooperatives.

  Cooperatives have to improve their infrastructure.

Materials Planning and Control

A material planning is part of inventory planning. Inventory planning in a manufacturing organization includes planning for materials planning for work-in-process and planning for finished goods. Inventory planning is basically material requirements planning (MRP).

Materials planning is "The scientific way of determining the requirements of raw materials, spares, and other item that go into meeting production needs within the economic investment policies'. It is the first activity and given a prominent place in the total inventory management set-up because planning for materials and working out a realistic budget not only help in motivating people but also serve as a control device. Materials planning function is a sub-system in the overall planning activity and its responsibility is to systematically determine the quantities and time schedule of the requirements. In fact, its role is to avoid a situation like for want of a nail a kingdom was lost".

Materials planning enable organizations to anticipate and not to react to the external and uncontrollable difficulties. The factors, which affect materials planning, can be classified in the following two categories:

1. *Micro factors:* The factors at micro level which affect materials planning are corporate objectives, plant capacity, technology, rejection rates, lead times, inventory levels, working capital, seasonability, delegation of powers, communication system, etc.
2. *Macro factors:* Some of the macro factors, which affect materials planning are the progress of the national economy and the price trends, international markets, business cycles, Fisical and monetary policies, taxation and foreign exchange regulations, government import policy, credit policy of banks etc.

Materials planning involves a number of things like the determination of quantity and quality, purchasing policies as well as procedures for purchasing materials. Likewise, controlling of materials is embodied in storekeeping, inventory valuation, as well as in handling materials within the plant. However, these aspects of materials planning and control are dealt with in the following way:

Quantity and Quality

The quantity of materials to be purchased is directly related o the sise of production run and is influenced by future sales programmes, available buying facilities, existing market conditions, and prevailing price trends of materials. For production purposes, the quantity may lead to delays and interruptions in manufacturing or to the total stoppage of work. On the other hand, too large quantities result in unnecessary tying of capital and other avoidable expenses due to obsolescence, deterioration of evaporation of materials as well as for storekeeping of excess materials. Between these two extremes, the correct quantity of materials is to be determined for all and every item of materials. For maintaining this correct quantity of materials is to be determined for all and every item of materials. For maintaining this correct quantity, the minimum and the maximum quantities are usually fixed for each item of the materials inventory. In addition, an ordering point is also decided upon so that inventory may not go down below the prescribed minimum because of the issue of the materials for production on the one hand, and of the time taken for producing new supplies on the other.

The quality of material is as important as the quantity is for production. Defective materials often lead to faulty production that requires rejections or scrapings. As rejections add to the cost of manufacturing, saving, made through the procurement of a cheaper and inferior quality of materials become a mere eye-wash. Besides, the cases of sales returns may go up and market standing of the enterprise may be affected because of the poor quality of products arising from defective materials. To avoid the risk of losing business and of incurring additional expenses, materials are to be procured in accordance with correct specifications. For ensuring the requisite quality of materials, specifications provide the standards of colour, texture, size, shape, grade or other like features. Materials are always tested in terms of these specifications before their transformation into finished products. Furthermore, accurate materials specifications help to avoid disputes or disagreements between the company and its vendors on quality grounds. Briefly, effective purchasing implies the procurement of quality materials at satisfactory prices, and it does not mean such materials that can be obtained at the lowest price.

Techniques of Materials Planning

A material planning is done at all stages and at all levels of management. The top management is usually engaged in planning for non-programmed decisions such as import policy, foreign exchange availability, credit squeeze and other monetary and fiscal policies. The middle-order management engages itself in planning for programmed decisions which are usually of routine nature such as hypothecating inventory for working capital, delivery schedules, quantity for requirements, etc.

Materials planning, however, are based on certain feedback information and reviews. Sales forecasting, production programming and materials planning are inter-connected. In fact, sales forecasting and production programming are two major functions, which normally precedes materials planning. There should be proper feedback information and periodic review in order to have better materials planning.

The techniques, which are usually used for materials planning, are—Bill of Materials Technique and Past Consumption Analysis Techniques.

A. Bill of Materials Technique

When an organization receives a work order or a production programme of the concern is finalized, a list of all the materials required for execution of the order or the concerned foreman prepares manufacturing of the product. The list of materials so prepared in known as Bill of Materials (BoM) which includes details such as quality, quantity, code number, drawing number and other necessary specifications. Thus, Bill of Materials is nothing but a document, which shows for a given component the list of materials, required, unit consumption, and location code.

BoM is the simplest technique of materials planning. BoM with required lead-time and necessary contingency provisions is drawn for each product or order, which eventually turns, into indents for procurement. It also acts as a guide to delivery and inventory requirements. A BoM, therefore, helps in keeping watch over the delivery of matching equipments, spare parts, components, and also over materials directly going into production. It enables the evaluation of the progress of the project undertaken and ensures the flow of required materials. A BoM is also helpful in avoiding the locking funds unnecessarily by proper scheduling the orders, delivery and arrival of materials. Such an avoidance of capital blockade saves and diverts the working capital and reduces the inventory carrying cost to a large extent.

B. Past Consumption Analysis Technique

Where materials are consumed on continuous basis the technique of past consumption analysis for materials planning is conveniently used by the organization. According to this technique future production is made on the basis of past consumption data, which is analyzed taking into consideration the past as well as future production plans. Statistical tools like mean, median, mode and standard deviation are used in analyzing the past consumption, projecting the future and tackling mild as well as wild fluctuations in consumption.

Self-learning Activity

Try to answer the following questions on your own:

1. Define materials management?
2. What are the types of materials required by an industry?
3. Describe the importance of materials management in cooperatives?

Summary

- Materials management is one of the functional areas of management.
- Materials management is an important function of management through which an organization would be able to control its cost of production and maintain quality in its products.
- Materials required by an industry ranges from raw materials, purchased parts, semi-processed materials, material supplies, and equipment.

- An organization could gain lot of benefits by means of efficient materials management.
- The first function of materials management is materials planning and control.
- While purchasing the materials, the planning function must give importance to quantity and quality considerations.
- Cooperatives, especially the producers' cooperatives, industrial cooperatives, and processing cooperatives must follow all the principles and techniques of materials management. To improve their operational efficiency and competitive power, cooperatives must follow the tools and techniques of materials management effectively.

Methods and Procedures of Purchasing 2

Methods of Purchasing

There are different methods employed in purchasing raw materials. The primary purchase methods are:

- centralized purchasing; and
- decentralized purchasing.

Each one of these methods can have the following subsidiary methods of buying:

- Bargain buying;
- Contract buying;
- Current Market buying; and
- Sub-contract buying.

All these methods will be discussed in turn.

Centralized Buying

In this method there is one central buying department for the whole organization. For plants located at different places, the central purchasing department arranges materials from all plants and branches, and these are processed centrally.

The merits of this system are as follows:

- Purchasing is a staff function subordinate to the production or line functions. It is easier to administer a staff function, on a uniform basis, from the central office.
- It is quite likely that different product lines or production departments require similar materials, and there may be

common suppliers to them. Hence, purchasing could be done effectively and more economically from one point instead of from several branches.

- As the availability of specialists is scarce, it is wise to have the services of those few available at a central office. Every plant or branch having its own purchasing department may not be able to have the services of purchasing specialists, and purchasing may thus be inefficient.
- Centralized buying will enable effective co-ordination and co-operation between the various branches or production plants. Mutual transfer of material from the surplus departments to deficit ones is easily possible through a centralized buying organ. The arguments advanced against centralized buying are given below:

Decentralized Buying

In this method every branch or plant is allowed to have an independent purchasing section. The arguments advanced in its favour are:

- Each branch or plant has a responsibility for its profitability performance. Every activity area, which affects profits, must, therefore, be under its direct authority. It is logical to allow every branch to make its own decisions regarding materials to be bought so that it can control the materials cost going into its output.
- Where the separate divisions or branches are quite big in size, purchases may be of large magnitude both in quantity and value. This circumstance would warrant allowing decentralized buying opportunity to the divisions.
- Local conditions of each branch may vary widely. It may not be possible for the centralized purchasing function to deal effectively with these factors. Besides, transportation problems may be really stupendous for

centralized buying and decentralized distribution of materials. Hence, each branch should have its own purchasing section.

- Good public relations could be fostered if the branches made purchases locally. This would bring about a closer and personal touch of the business with the local business community.

Bargain Buying

This method of buying is usually adopted for buying basic raw materials of industry on a speculative basis. Buying is done with a view to making huge profits out of fluctuations in prices of raw materials. Bargains are entered into on the basis of anticipations about prices. If the anticipations come out true, buying is successful. They may not also prove true, and, therefore, this method entails risks too. A policy decision should be made by top-management before this method of buying is practiced, and a top official should be deputed as in charge of this method.

Contract Buying

Under this method long-term contracts are entered into with suppliers for making available regular supplies of materials to the business. Such contracts have cancellation and revision clauses allowing either party the opportunity to terminate the agreement after a suitable notice to the other party.

This method has several benefits. It avoids the necessity of having to buy materials in bulk and store them for a long period, with the attendant risks of wastage of stocks as also wastage of interest on capital locked up in stocks. It also allows the benefit of getting special rate and terms of contract because of its long-term basis and the sense of stability secured by the supplier. On being assured of a long and continuous period of supply, comprehensive long-term production plans can be launched.

This method may, engender a sense of complacency and in action on the part of the purchasing department. It may cease to be alert about new and changing conditions in the materials market, about the availability of new substitutes, etc. There is also the possible danger of allowing favouritism, with attendant consequences, etc. to grow if certain suppliers are put on such contracts over long periods without break.

Current Market Buying

Here buying proceeds as and when the need arises. Quotations and tenders are invited and compared, and orders are placed with the most appropriate supplier. A well-organized system operates for indicating when stocks reach the ordering level so that new orders are placed in time. Other indicators like minimum stock, maximum stock, optimum order quantity, etc. also exist.

This method has the advantage of allowing the buying department to use its judgment and discretion in keeping the buying policy in step with changing market conditions. It has, therefore, to maintain an ever-alert watch on market trends about prices, substitutes, etc.

There is however, the difficulty of obtaining the right balance between too frequent orders of small quantity and the attendant procurement and procedural expenses on the one hand, and too few bulk orders with associated costs of storage and locking up of capital on the other. The appropriate order quantity and frequency must be found out to make an efficient use of this method.

Sub-contract Buying

This method is sometimes adopted as a solution to make-or-buy decisions. Some semi-processed or semi-manufactured ingredients may be sub-contracted to other producers instead of manufacturing them within one's own plant.

The advantages are many. A plant may face temporary shortages in capacity, which does not warrant permanent capital investments. In such cases, the sub-contracting method may be used to procure supplies. Again, the plant to which the subcontract is given may have specialized techniques in manufacturing those supplies or parts. It is wise to use such suppliers who would be able to give the requirements of a better quality at a lower price.

There are disadvantages also. The sub-contractor may fail to give regular and good quality supplies, and thus the production schedule of the plant may be disrupted. If the plant wants to keep its manufacturing ingredients secret, contracting out some parts to outsiders may frustrate this objective.

Reciprocal Buying

The policy of reciprocal buying is based on the idea of give and take on the part of buyers and suppliers. It involves the choosing of those suppliers who purchases, or give encouragements to purchasing, products of the buyer. These buying practices provide the connecting link between the sale of products and the purchase of materials. Reciprocal buying increases sales, fosters the growth of close relationships, and simplifies the purchasing procedure. On the other hand, reciprocal buying makes the purchasing activities of secondary importance to the sale of products, prevents the procurement of best supplies from the market, and gives premium on the inefficiencies of both buyers and suppliers.

Number of Vendors

The number of sources from which materials should be obtained is another field for policy formulation in the work of materials planning. The question is whether materials are to be procured from one or two sources, or from a number of sources. The one-source procurement policy provides means of dependable deliveries, better service facilitates from the vendor, satisfactory trade relationship and of buying quality materials. It has special importance in obtaining specialized materials and carries the advantage of securing materials on credit terms. But the risk of non-delivery is inherently present in one - source supply because of the possible strikes; lockouts or other forced work stoppages in the supplier's firm. Moreover, although prices are likely to become reasonable, it does not allow reaping the benefit of competitive bidding. To overcome these defects of one-source supply, many companies have developed multi-source procurement policy.

The advantages of multiple source include:

(a) stable and continued supply of materials despite strikes, accidents, floods, fires or other calamities in suppliers' plants;

(b) quality and price of materials are always compatible with current market conditions and developments; and

(c) sales can be improved through trade relationships with many suppliers under a policy of reciprocal buying.

Procedure for Purchasing Materials

The purchasing procedure varies from case to case and is designed to suit the specific requirements of a particular enterprise. In any case, the major steps involves in the purchasing procedure of all enterprises may be stated as follows:

- Authorizing purchase by a designated person is the first step required in buying activities. Usually, for recurring items that are fully covered by the purchasing programme the stores section initiates action. But for special items of materials or supplies, the manager in charge of inventory control takes the purchasing decisions. Whoever may be the authorized person for making decision on the purchase of materials, all decisions must indicate the quality and quantity of materials as well as the expected time and place of delivery.
- Obtaining quotations from suppliers is the second step involved in purchasing. Quotations and delivery periods are secured from a number of concerns through interviewing their salesmen or making direct

communications with them. Where price variations are not important and competitive bidding is deemed unnecessary, quotations are not usually obtained. Instead, the selection of actual suppliers is made from considerations like promptness and reliability of delivery.

- Placing of orders is recognized as the third step in a purchasing procedure. After comparing quotations and terms of delivery, the actual order is placed with one or more suppliers. In the purchase order, certain details are included for providing requisite information and guidance to the supplier, viz., the name and address of the vendor, place and time of delivery, basic price and other charge for carrying materials, the grounds for rejections and the penalty for failure to deliver in time.
- Follow up and inspection becomes the last step in purchasing materials. Follow-up is an act of pursuance for reminding the supplier in fulfilling his terms of sale. When materials are delivered, they are inspected as to their quantity, quality and other specifications contained in the purchase order.

Control Over Materials

In view of the material cost being an important component of the total cost, adequate control over materials may be discussed under the following three phases:

A. Storekeeping of materials

Proper storekeeping makes it a task to see that capital is not tied up in excess or superfluous materials on the one hand, and that production is not hampered for want of materials on the other. To achieve this object of economy and prudence, levels of the minimum and the maximum quantity and fixed in respect of each item of materials inventory. Storekeeping involves the maintenance of quantity figures within the prescribed levels for all and every item of materials. However, to maintain these quantity levels, an ordering point is established with reference to the rate of materials consumption and the time required for further procurement. For replenishment purposes, the ordering point provides a guide as to when the purchase order should be released. Furthermore, storekeeping is also concerned with safekeeping of materials so as to prevent their loss, deterioration, depreciation or damages. But storekeeping requires some expenses of its own. It is estimated in responsible quarters that storekeeping absorbs a cost varying from 10 per cent to 20 per cent of the materials cost. And this cost of storekeeping represents a sheer waste where excess materials are procured much in advance of the production programme. Rigid adherence to the maximum quantity level has thus a salutary effect on the reduction of storing cost.

Receipts and issue of materials is a sphere of storekeeping work that requires an utmost care. Without being supported by a written record and a proper authorization, no amount of materials should be allowed to come in or to go away. There are two possible sources of materials receipt. Materials are mostly received form outside vendors. But unused and surplus materials on the part of a section or a shop of the plant also be returned to the stores. In both the cases, receipt of materials must be supported by a written account of the items. Likewise, for issuing materials, there should be a properly authorized staff for issuing request on from the foremen or the superintendent. For the maintenance of quantitative record of materials, a rule is commonly established to the effect that all shops must obtain their materials directly from the store, not from the surplus materials of a neighbouring shop.

B. Inventory valuation

The traditional basis of inventory valuation is to take the market price or cost price of materials which ever is lower. Because of this rough and ready practice employed in valuing materials, it does not find favour with many managers who want to replace it other methods. There are four methods available for the purpose viz., *(a)* first in, first out (fifo);

(b) last in, first out (lifo); *(c)* standard cost; and *(d)* cumulative average. Under the method of first, the first of materials purchased to be first, and on depletes of the first lot is lot, issues are made from the second lot, third lot and so on. Lot-wise prices become the basis of materials valuation. However, this method does not provide a satisfactory basis of valuation. During rising prices, materials are undervalued and have no touch with the realities of market conditions. Similarly, during falling prices, materials are overvalued. Under the method of last in, first out, materials are supposed to be issued in a reverse order, commencing from the last lot. Arguments in support of this method are that as incoming materials are usually placed at the top of a stack or a heap, and as materials are issued from the top of the stack, the last lot of materials is actually used first for production purposes. Like the first method, it too has limitations. During rising prices it overvalues materials, while under valuation is to be found at the time of falling prices.

Under the third method, a standard cost is ascertained for each item of materials from study, analysis and past experience. Once determined, the same cost is used for the valuation of all materials issued in respect of an individual item. Any discrepancy between the standard cost and the actual price is usually adjusted in the profit and loss account under the title of 'Difference in Inventory valuation'.

It is an easy method to use no doubt, but it cannot be relied upon at the time of wide price fluctuations. In the cumulative average method, unit cost for each item is calculated by dividing the aggregate value of materials in hand by the number of units pertaining to a particular item. On the basis of prevailing unit costs, materials are valued at the time of their issue. This is the best of the four methods; but it requires fresh calculation of unit const, whenever further quantity of an item is acquired at different prices.

C. Handling of materials

Materials handling within the plant add to the cost of production in several ways. Besides the indirect labour cost involved in materials handling, there are costs of damaged materials, employee accidents and pilferage. The indirect labour cost of materials handling goes up tremendously in those cases where traveling and backtracking of materials are required over long distances. The flow or movement of materials is related to the type of plant layout. For effective materials handling, layout is to be designed with an eye to the flow of production and consequently to the flow of materials. Many types of mechanical equipment are available for efficient and economical handling of materials. It is the task of materials management to see that proper equipments are utilized in appropriate cases. By the use of mechanical equipments, the cost of materials handling can be reduced substantially.

Principles of Purchasing

The basic objective of the purchasing function is to ensure continuity of supply of raw materials, spare parts and other items and at the same time reduce the ultimate cost of the finished goods. The objective is not so much to procure the raw materials at the lowest price but to reduce the cost of the final product. For ensuring this the necessary parameters are discussed as follows:

Right Price: Right price need not be the lowest price as usually understood. The tender system of buying is normally used in public sector organizations. The objective should be to identify the lowest responsible bidder and no the lowest bidder. The price can be kept low by proper planning and not by rush buying. Price negotiation also helps to determine the right prices.

Right Quality: In order to determine the quality of a product sampling schemes are quite useful. The quality particulars are obtained from the indents and experience indicates that the substantial portion of the indents prepared by the user departments are invariably incomplete. The objective of purchasing is to ensure continuity of supply the time at which the material is provided to the user department assumes great importance.

Right Time: The purchase manager should have lead time information for all products. Lead time is eth total time elapsed between the recognition of the need of an item till the item actually arrives and is provided for use. While determining the purchases, the buyer has to consider emergency situations like floods, strikes, etc. Howêver rush purchase should be resorted to only in exceptional circumstances.

*Right Sources:*The source of the material should be dependable and capable of supplying items of uniform quality. Techniques such as value analysis will enable the buyer to locate the right material. Specifying the right place of delivery, say, head office or works would often minimize the handling and transportation costs. Packaging forms an important aspect in the cost of an item.

Right Quantity: The right quantity is an important parameter in buying. Economic Order Quantity (E.O.Q), Economic Purchase Quantity (E.P.Q.), Fixed quantity systems will serve as broad guidelines. The buyer has to adopt separate policies and procedures for capital and consumer items.

Negotiation: Negotiation for prices has been accepted as a policy by some material managers. It is an art of embodying sophisticated tactics. A successful negotiator has to possess the qualities of patience, persuasiveness, clear thinking, logical analysis, optimism knock of getting along with people, ability to plan and be 'thick skinned'.

Factors to be considered in purchasing

There are several factors influencing the purchasing. They are internal and external to the organization. A careful analysis of these factors will facilitate the work of the purchasing department.

1. Ability to maintain prompt and regular supply of stores

The purchasing department must have the detailed production and plant utilization schedules and must programme its activities accordingly. Appropriate timing of purchases is crucial to the prevention of stoppages, owing to short supply of materials. Not only will production be lost, overhead will also remain loss.

2. Minimizing capital locked up in stores

Buying stores at the appropriate time also implies that huge stocks are not piled up. Capital blocked in stocks prevents the use of capital along more profitable channels or may even lead to the abandonment of certain projects. An ensured even flow of stores does not allow stocks to exceed certain maximum limits. Cooperatives, who are starving for funds are not afford to lock their capital.

3. Economic ordering

Economic ordering quantity is a problem associated with inventory control. It will be a quantity, which is able to secure the optimum price, is able to ensure continuous production, and at the same time, prevent loss due to high stocks and consequent storage and other expenses. A model should be built up relating all these variables; the economic ordering quantity should be calculated.

4. Establishing close liaison with suppliers

Value analysis users recommend a regular meeting with suppliers these days. These meetings will enable the suppliers to help the purchasers to meet the latter's value requirements. As a matter of fact, if suppliers are carefully explained the real function of the item they are supplying at present, they may come out with a better alternative for the purpose at a lesser cost.

5. Stimulating competition between suppliers

This is a useful way of securing lower prices and better quality. But this method may be used not without some precautions. If the intention is always just to set one supplier against the other, the real desire to purchase being absent, then such a buyer may be left without any seller must be convinced of such genuineness.

6. Provision of adequate check upon receipt of supplies

Suppliers get orders from the purchase department, but the goods are received at the goods inwards section and then passed through the inspection department. The purchasing department must, therefore, plan a coordinated scheme of verifying that receipts are in conformity with the quality and quantity ordered for.

Forecasting

As planning involves future, forecasting has become an essential element in planning. Based on the previous experience the manager has to plan the future. Forecasting is necessary to prepare the organization for any future uncertainty and to meet the future challenges. Forecasting can check the wastages and keep the tempo of the organization in terms of its turnover, profit etc. Drucker holds that "management has no choice but to anticipate the future, to mould it and balance short range and long range goals. Any management decision must therefore contain provision for change, adaptation and salvage".

Forecasting has an important role to play in materials management. A materials manager has to forecast the future trend in order to purchase the materials at a cheaper cost and with adequate quantity.

Factors that influence forecasting

- *Government policies:* Government policies towards taxation, regulation, etc must be viewed property.
- *Change in population:* can change the demand and supply of goods.
- *Change in fashion, tastes, etc.:* when society changes tastes of the people a change. When fashion changes new products give way to old. A company must predict such changes.

Criteria for Good Forecast

The following are the criteria for good forecast:

- Forecasting must be accurate.
- Forecast must be timely.
- The data must be applicable to the solution of specific problems.
- The data should be inexpensive to collect and to analyze in terms of the results.
- The forecast should be intelligible to the management.

Areas of Forecasting

- *Economic development:* The economic conditions of the country as well as those of the whole world would have significant effect on the operations of an organization. This will include predictions relating to GNP, currency strength, industrial expansion, job market, balance of payments etc.
- *Technological forecasts:* These forecasts predict the new technological developments that may change the operations of an organization. An organization keeps up to date with new technological developments and readily adopts new methods to improve performance.
- *Competition forecasts:* It is necessary to predict as to what strategies our competitors would be employing. The competitor may be working to employ a different marketing strategy for the same product or bringing out a substitute for the product which could be cheaper and easily acceptable.
- *Social forecasts:* These forecasts involve predicting changes in the consumer tastes, demands and attitudes.
- *Other forecasts:* Other necessary forecasts are predictions about new laws, political events, labour supplies etc. These are all critical areas with impacts on the planning process.

Forecasting Techniques

There are basically two broad categories of forecasting techniques. These are:

(i) Qualitative techniques;

(ii) Quantitative techniques.

A. ***Qualitative forecasting techniques:*** These techniques are primarily based upon judgment and intuition and especially when sufficient information and data is not available so that complex quantitative techniques cannot be use omen widely used qualitative methods are:

(a) *Jury of executive opinion:* This is a method by which the relevant opinions of experts are taken, combined and averaged. These opinions could be taken on an individual basis or there could be a brain storming group session in which all members participate in generating new ideas that can later be evaluated for their feasibility and profitability.

(b) *Opinions of the sales person:* The sales people being closer to consumers can estimate future sales in their own territories, more accurately. Based on these and the opinions of sales managers, a reasonable trend of the future sales can be calculated. These forecasts are good for short range planning since sales people are not sufficiently sophisticated to predict long-term trends.

(c) *Consumers expectations:* This method involves a survey of the customers as to their future needs. This method is especially useful where the industry serves a limited market. Based on the future needs of the customers a general overall forecast for the demand can be made.

(d) *The Delphi method:* The Delphi method, originally developed by Rank Corporation in 1969 of forecast military events, has become a useful tool in other areas also. It is basically a more formal version of the jury of opinion method. A panel of experts is given a situation and asked to make initial predictions, in the basis of a prescribed

questionnaire, these experts develop written opinions. These responses are analysed and summarized and submitted back to the panel for further considerations. All these responses are anonymous so that no member is influenced by others opinions. This process is repeated until a consensus is obtained.

B. *Quantitative forecasting techniques:* These techniques use statistical analysis and other mathematical models to predict future events, primarily based upon past activities. They are as follows:

(a) *Time series analysis:* This analysis is based on the assumption that activities are good indication of future activities. The past trends are extended into the future barring any unforeseen circumstances. These techniques are fairly sophisticated and require experts to use these methods. The method is quite accurate where future is expected to be similar to past.

(b) *Causal models:* These models are more complex in nature and involve inter-relationships of many variables tied together in a quantitative model. These models are primarily used to predict economic trends and are based on a multitude of factors, probabilities and assumptions. No matter what model or method is used, forecasting basically rests on human judgment. Even the most sophisticated models have to be interpreted by humans.

(c) *Break even analysis:* Break-even analysis is also a very important quantitative forecasting tool. It is a composite of various elements liken total revenue, fixed cost, variable cost and total cost.

(d) *Budget:* Budget also helps to forecast things. It is through budget, and organization can give expression to the plan in terms of costs and revenues.

(e) *Scheduling:* It is part of an action plan and it is a process of establishing a time sequence for the work to be done.

(f) *Inventory:* A technique that is in vogue is economic order quantity (EOQ). Its object is to ensure maintenance of an adequate inventory on hand at the lowest total cost to the organization.

(g) *Linear Programming:* is also used for forecasting.

Forecasting in Cooperatives

All cooperatives, especially producer's cooperatives and processing cooperatives need to concentrate on forecasting. Forecasting is needed in cooperatives for the following reasons:

- To face competition from public and private sector.
- To improve their own operations efficiency and to reduce their cost.
- To move with the changing technology and to adopt latest technology.
- To meet the future needs of member's cooperatives have to forecast.
- To achieve self-reliance in resources and to be free from external interferences.

Self-learning Activity

Try to answer the following questions on your own:

1. What is bargain buying?
2. Discuss the procedures for purchasing materials?
3. Explain the principles of purchasing?
4. Describe qualitative forecasting techniques?

Summary

- There are various methods of purchasing, like centralized purchasing, decentralized purchasing, contract buying, current market buying, and sub-contract buying. Each method has it own merits and limitations.

- While purchasing the materials, organizations follow certain scientific principles. Purchasing orders are made by an authorized person who is highly responsible to the job. Goods are purchased after verifying the price, quality, etc through quotations.
- Important principles of purchasing are to purchase the commodities at right price, right quality, right time, right source, and right quantity.
- Like all other functions, materials department must also forecast their future needs for their requirements.
- The forecasting techniques are classified into quantitative forecasting techniques and qualitative forecasting techniques.
- Cooperatives must also forecast their future requirements in order to produce the goods at a cheaper cost, to face competition and to improve their operational efficiency.

3 Supplier Selection

Vendor Rating/Selection of Suppliers

An organization has to take care in selecting the suppliers for materials. A supplier must be honest in his dealings and must supply the materials in time with prescribed quality. There is a difference between source selection and vendor rating. While selecting a source the major factors that were considered were the probable sources' capacities, capabilities, organization, finances, location and performance in the market, whereas, while rating a vendor more importance is given to his actual performance in the transaction with emphasis on quality, quantity, ability to stick to schedules and the financial implications of the contract. In vendor rating, weights are given to these various factors and the vendor's performance is evaluated on the basis of these factors.

Features of Vendor Rating

- The rating method must be logical and scientific to such an extent that the vendor himself can be informed of the methodology and can be fed-back on his failings.
- Vendor rating is not a one-way process. Just as the buyer rates the performance of his various suppliers, the seller also rates the buyer according to whether he is regular in his payments, his adherence to contractual obligations and the mutual trust that can be built between the two. In fact this mutual rating of each other's interactions can foster better buyer-seller relationship.

- An efficient vendor rating system obtains the best vendor for the organization, which saves both time and money. The objective of the vendor rating system is to obtain the best value for the money spent on purchases.
- A major advantage of vendor rating is that it rates the entire performance of the vendor and is not guided by a tunnel vision. This also gives the purchaser additional information on the capabilities of the vendor with regard to know-how, testing, transport, contractual willingness, etc and he can use them to his advantage whenever he has a particular need.

The Technique of Vendor Rating

It is a weighted average method for finding the effectiveness of a vendor. The vendor's performance in meeting the quality, delivery and price standards set by the buyer are assessed systematically and as objectively as possible, though a subjective element in measuring the vendors' attitude and behavior is not precluded. An attempt is made to computer the rating accurately and regularly so that the purchasing activities can be guided along the right tract. The primary use of vendor rating is to objectively compare the performances of vendors and improve the relations with the better performers. The ratings can also be used as a feedback to the vendors. They should be informed of the measuring system and the way they are scoring. To inculcate a competitive spirit the scores of other vendors may be mentioned after properly disguising their identities.

Rating of Vendors

The major factors that are considered for vendor rating are quality as measured by rejection, adherence to quantity, time schedule of supplies and the price. The vendors are rated objectively on these three scales. The rating on each scale is multiplies by its weight age factor and the sum of these products gives the overall rating.

A. Ratings on a Quality Scale

Quite expectedly, quality rating should be a function of the percentage of lots rejected at chosen levels of acceptable quality. We can measure it directly from the percentage of lots accepted or from the sampling plan taking into account the percent defective, and the sample size or based on the cost of inspection. It can be noted that the first method is the easiest while the latter two methods require more computation.

B. Ratings on a Quantity Scale

Unless the vendor supplies the materials in the quantities contracted ad according to the schedule, the buying organization will be at a loss due to lack of materials. Therefore, adherence to quantity and delivery schedules is an important rating factor. This performance can be split into one measure for adhering to time schedule and another for adhering to quantity schedule.

Rating for adhering to time schedule

$$= \frac{\text{Number of deliveries made on the scheduled date}}{\text{Total number of scheduled deliveries in the period}}$$

Rating for adhering to quantity schedule

$$= \frac{\text{Number of correct lot sizes delivered}}{\text{Total number of scheduled deliveries}}$$

In these cases we can fix an upper and lower limit from the contracted time schedule and lot size quantity to compute whether the deliveries have been in time and according to the quantity required.

C. Price Rating Scale

The actual price paid can be compared with a standard price and the rating can be measured from this. In this case we have to give credit to those vendors who accept delayed payments since in effect they are partly bearing the organization's financing costs.

These are the three major ratings, which can be measured sufficiently objectively. Factors like sellers' attitudes, behavior, treatment and negotiability can be measured only on a subjective basis. A workable strategy would be to obtain the objective rating first and if there are some doubts then the subjective ratings can be used.

Interpersonal Relations

The purchasing Manager is in the unenviable position of having to please everybody. But if he is to be effective in his profession he cannot afford to antagonize either his suppliers or his consumers or the finance section, which passes the bills. He cannot afford to loose his cool when confronted with conflicting interests nor can he take the side of one party against another. In fact his position as a buffer depends on his quality of absorbing the bickering from all directions. An ability to move with others will be of great advantage to him. His role can be equated to a balancing force, which is required to keep the resultant of the three forces of the seller, consumer and financier in balance.

Interpersonal Relationship with Various Groups

1. Buyer-seller Relations

The relations between a buyer and a seller cannot be confined to legalities. If either party proceeds on such a premise, they will find to their disadvantage the futility of following such a policy. It would be to their mutual benefit if they recognize the fact that they are in a cooperative situation rather than in a conflicting situation. It would be better for them to work with each other's strengths rather than at each other's weaknesses. The effectiveness of both parties will improve mutual trust and a give and take approach can be built up.

A good buyer-seller relationship can be made mutually beneficial. At times the seller can suggest technical improvements to the buyer.; The buyer may be able to help the seller when he faces some technical or procurement hurdles. It is imperative for the buyer to continuously evaluate his relations with the sellers and plug any loopholes anywhere. Nothing is more effective in interpersonal relations than a stitch in time.

2. Purchaser-consumer Relations

The purchaser is functionally service agent of the consumer, who tends to measure his performance not by the continuous supply of materials but the stock outs. The consumer here is; the production or maintenance departments who consume the purchased materials. Bu maintaining a proper service level and procuring the right quantity at the right time much of the ill will can be converted to goodwill.

A positive approach will be not to depend too much on bureaucratic and routine procedures. Instead, informal channels of information should be tapped. A rapport can be easily established if the employees of the purchasing division adopt a helping attitude towards the consumers.

3. Purchaser-controller Relations

The transaction of the purchasing department are verified and controlled by the finance. The quality control department verifies the quality of the materials purchased and their acceptance depends on their remarks. This can lead to a lot of friction. The main cause is a lack of information on the exact quality requirements, the tolerances and the minimum acceptable levels. Therefore, if a genuine attempt is made to reduce this lack of knowledge many of the difficulties can be ironed out.

Types of Evaluation Needed for Vendor Rating

The type of evaluation required to determine supplier capability varies with the nature, complexity, and value of the purchase to be made. It also varies with the buyer's knowledge of the firms being considered for the order. For many uncomplicated, low value purchases and examination of the information already available in the purchasing department is sufficient. For complex, high-value purchases, additional evaluation steps are necessary.

These steps can include visits to the plants of carefully selected vendors, their financial managerial and service capabilities. For an extremely difficult purchase, a vendor evaluation conference can be held at the buyer's plant. From the conference discussion of the purchase, it is usually easy to identify which vendors understand the complexities of the purchase and which do not. By eliminating those who do not, the search for the right supplier is further narrowed. Lee and Dobler explain the following evaluation methods.

Plant Visits

To obtain first-hand information about the adequacy of a vendor's manufacturing facilities and technical know-how; a buyer should visit the vendor's plant. Depending on the importance of the visit, the company may send representatives from only purchasing and engineering: of it may also include some combination of representation from finance, production, quality control, and industrial relations, occasionally the management may also participate in the visit and its evaluation.

Check-Sheet For Vendor Rating

1. *Reliability*
   (*a*) Is the supplier reputable, stable and financially strong?
   (*b*) Are the supplier's integrity and ability above doubt?
   (*c*) Is the supplier going along with product improvement?
   (*d*) Is the supplier's competitive strength as to price, quality, etc. proved by past experience?
2. *Technical capabilities*
   (*a*) Can the supplier provide assistance as to application engineering?

(b) Can the supplier provide assistance as to analytical engineering?
(c) Can the supplier provide design assistance?
(d) Can the supplier handle special needs and contribute to improve product efficiency\basic process?

3. *Convenience*
(a) Can the supplier help reducing acquisition costs through personal visits, telephone calls, incoming inspections, rejection of defects, spoilage, etc.?
(b) Can he offer other related products?
(c) Is he qualified to help in solving difficult problems?
(d) Does the supplier package his product conveniently?

4. *Availability*
(a) Does the supplier assure delivery in time?
(b) Are his stocks locally available, or at short notice?
(c) Can he plan his supply to minimize inventory?
(d) Can he be depended on for a steady flow of materials?

5. *After-sales service*
(a) Does the supplier have a service organization?
(b) Is an emergency service available?
(c) Are parts available, when needed?

6. *Sales assistance*
(a) Can the supplier be building mutual markets?
(b) Will he recommend our products?
(c) Does the use of supplier's product enhance appearance of our products?

2. Financial Condition

Preliminary investigation of a vendor's financial condition can often eliminate the expense of further investigation. Investigation of financial statements and credit ratings can reveal whether a vendor is clearly incapable of performing satisfactorily. Financial stability is essential for suppliers to assure continuity of supply and reliability of product quality.

3. Management

A well-managed firm seldom experiences the instability that result from their continual labour problems, goods it strives continuously to reduce it costs. Such a company can be a good supplier. Good business management, must be blended with technical competence to ensure that a firm has the ability to be a good sources of supply in the full sense of the term.

4. Service

Good service always means delivering on time, treating special orders specially, filing back orders promptly, and informing, buyers in advance of impending price changes or developing shortages. In the aggregate, good service means that a supplier will take every reasonable action to ensure the smooth flow of purchased materials between the seller and the buyer.

Post Selection Problems

A. Assistance to Suppliers

Once an order or a contract is awarded, the relationship between the buyer and the seller legally becomes a contractual one. Unfortunately with the passage of time, this situation frequently produces buyer complacency. Too often buyers feel that consummating a contract with a carefully selected supplier ends their major responsibility, at least for the time being. Such buyers feel that the supplier is legally bound to perform and that using departments will inform buyer whenever a supplier fails in this obligation.

To progressive buyer, nothing short of supplier success is buyer success. To help assure such success, effective buyers will make available to a new supplier the research, management, and technical services of their own companies. They will instruct new suppliers on the buying company's methods of operation, its special problems, and its known areas of weakness. This information enables a new supplier to contribute its knowledge and skills to help solve the buying firm's problems, For other than off-the-shelf items, both buyer and seller realize that total company capabilities are involved, not just commodities.

B. Supplier Performance Ratings

After sources of supply are selected, their performance must be evaluated. Evaluation provides the buyer with objective information to use in subsequent negotiations and in making future source selections.

The National Association of Purchasing Management of USA investigates three evaluation plans. Each of these plans is reviewed briefly. They are the categorical plan, the weighted-point plan, and the cost-ratio plan.

- *Categorical Plan:* Under this plan, personnel from various divisions maintain informal evaluation records. Individuals involved traditionally include personnel from purchasing, engineering, quality control, inspection, and receiving. For each major supplier, each person prepares a list of performance factors, which are important to him. At a monthly meeting, each major supplier is evaluated against each evaluator's list of factors. Each supplier is then assigned an overall group evaluation, usually expressed in simple categorical terms, such as 'preferred, 'neutral, 'or 'unsatisfactory'.
- *The Weighted-point Plan:* Under this plan, the performance factors to be evaluated (often only quality, service, and price) are 'weights'. After performance factors have been selected and weighted a specific procedure must be developed for measuring actual supplier performance on each individual factor. Supplier performance on each factor must be expressed in quantitative terms. To

determine a supplier's overall rating, each factor weight is multiplied by the supplier's overall rating, each factor weight is multiplied by the supplier's corresponding performance number; these products (for each factor) are then totaled to get the supplier's final rating for the time period in question.

- *Cost-ratio Plan:* This plan evaluates supplier performance by using the various tools, of 'standard cost' analysis that business people traditionally use in evaluating a wide variety of service operation. When using this `plan, the buying firm's costs uniquely associated with quality, delivery, and service are determined for each supplier. Each of these costs is then converted to a cost ratio. These three cost ratios are then totaled for each supplier, producing the suppliers overall cost ratios.

The Problem of Late Deliveries

The buyer, having placed a purchase order with an approved supplier, is dependent upon that supplier to fulfill his delivery promises. While 'penalty' and 'break' clauses can be written into an order, they are often difficult to enforce, and by the time that it is known that the delivery will be late, it is often too late to renegotiate the order with a new supplier. Dr.E.N. Hague, then Purchasing Manager for the Shell Petroleum Company Ltd, listed 'Do's' and 'Don'ts' for buyers.

Do

- ❖ Use clear and complete specifications.
- ❖ Keep demands for 'Rush' delivery to a workable minimum.
- ❖ Keep records of the delivery performance of suppliers.
- ❖ Try to find good alternative suppliers to those whose delivery performances are consistently bad.
- ❖ Keep abreast of suppliers current range of delivery times.

- ❖ Get to know supplier's policy as regards stocking of raw materials.
- ❖ Visit suppliers regularly.
- ❖ Restrict the number of really top level approaches to suppliers with delivery grouses.
- ❖ Consider the elimination of customer's inspection.
- ❖ Pay suppliers promptly.

Don't

- ❖ Nominate a delivery time, which is clearly unrealistic.
- ❖ Build in safety factors.
- ❖ Expect 'improved' delivery promises to be met consistently.
- ❖ Give suppliers a ready excuse for late delivery.
- ❖ Expedite suppliers whose delivery promises are consistently kept.
- ❖ Leave finished goods lying around in suppliers' works.

The Purchase Order

The purchase order is a contractual document, which may well bind the originating company to a considerable expenditure. It is most important therefore that it should be clear and unambiguous. The following statements:

- 'Price to be agreed'
- 'Delivery as soon as possible'
- 'Of good quality'
- 'Of normal commercial quality'
- 'As previously supplied'
- 'As discussed'

and other of a similar nature should never be used, since they are too loose to be useful, and can cause considerable difficulties later when goods are delivered of a quality other than that required, or at a date later than useful.

The purchase order should carry at least the following information:

- Name and address of originating company.
- Name and address of receiving company.
- Identifying number.
- Quantity of product required.
- Full description and/or specification of product required
- Price agreed between buyer and vendor.
- Delivery agreed between buyer and vendor.
- Cost allocation—this is for internal use.
- Delivery instructions-this for internal use.
- Buyer's signature and standing in company.
- Company's conditions of business.

The authority to sign purchase orders is usually restricted to one or two persons within the company, and limitations may be imposed as to the amount of expenditure, which may be incurred by a signatory.

Steps for Effective Purchasing

The following steps are taken for carrying out effective purchasing:

- Pre-purchase System
- Ordering System
- Post purchase System

Pre-purchase System

The salient features of the system are initiating the purchase through requisitions, requirement programmes, selection of suppliers, obtaining quotations, and evaluating them.'

Requisitions: The department concerned is needed of a material usually presents a completed requisition form. Requisition may be made by any one in the concerned department. However, it has to be countersigned by a senior officer. In an organization only a limited number of officers are empowered to countersign the requisition as it amounts to authorization of the expenditure. Purchase department must have the list of such officers so as to check the validity of the purchase requisition. There is a delegation of authority in authorizing a requisition. This is expressed in terms of the financial limits unto which an officer can authorize a requisition. It is important to note that capital equipments can not be requisitioned in this manner.

Travelling Requisitions: The document is widely used for requisitioning items that are required frequently in bulk quantities over a long period. The requisition travels from the requisitioning department to the purchased department often. During each stage a purchase order is initiated. Specifications, supplier details are written permanently and provisions for entering date, quantity required, names of requisitioners and authorizer are available. This reduces paper work and eases the operation. Standardized clerical systems can be devised and the bulk of the work can then be efficiently handled.

Enquiries

Many organizations often invite suppliers to quote rates for supply of materials. For this purpose a standard format is used which is similar to a purchase order in all respects except that words as 'this is only a request for quotation' or 'this is not a purchase order,' are printed so as to ensure that the suppler does not construe the request for quotation as a firm order'.

Ordering System

Having selected the supplier and the rates agreed, the buyer places the purchase order on the supplier, expressing the terms and conditions. The purchase order once accepted becomes a biding contract. The details that are normally finished in a purchase order are listed below:

- Purchase order reference number;
- Description of the materials and detailed specifications;
- Quantity required and delivery schedule;
- Price and discounts;
- Shipping instructions;
- Location where the materials are to be shipped;
- Signature of the Materials Manager who can authorize the purchase order; and
- Detailed terms and conditions (as a common practice these are printed at the back of the purchase order).

Written acceptance from the supplier is obtained. Normally five or six copies are prepared. The original is sent to the supplier with an acknowledgement copy which is expected to come back to the materials management department for following and attending to queries. One copy is sent to the receiving department intimating when the consignment is expected so as to facilitate identification. Another copy goes to the indentor for information. The last copy goes to the finance department for subsequent matching with the invoice of the supplier and goods received notes for payment.

Post-purchase System

This includes follow-up procedures, receipt and checking invoices. Generally certain priorities are established for follow-up. Only critical items require continuous follow-up. For fast moving items follow-up can be initiated whenever the stock levels depletes to one months consumption. For slow moving items also norms can be established. A few organizations also have decentralized inspection facilities for on the spot inspection and acceptance.

Receipt: A systematic record of the consignments received carrier details and descriptions are to maintained in chronological sequence to help in quick identification of materials so that inspection can be arranged prior to acceptance. Many organizations have separate central receiving section for this purpose.

Invoice Checking: The supplier normally sends the invoice for the materials supplied for payment. It is essential that this invoice is matched against the receipt details, quantity accepted and rejected so that payment can be made within the discount period or provisions be made which will keep in funds planning. Normally invoice are sent to the buyer's finance department. A close coordination between the finance and materials management departments is necessary.

Make or Buy Decisions

Companies producing goods from assembled parts usually earn more profit on components they make "in-house" than on components they buy from outside suppliers. Nevertheless, if they tried to produce all their own needed components, they would probably lose money. This is because they would lack the diversified skills and facilities needed to do an effective job.

Some items, such as supplies and low-valued components that are not within the main line of expertise of the firm, are obvious candidates for purchase.

Make or buy decisions made on a day-to-day basis relate largely to the use of existing capacity. They may require the joint evaluation of the purchasing, operations, engineering, accounting, and other departments of the firm because numerous considerations come into play. One approach is to first establish the economic feasibility and then follow with a consideration of more value-based, 'less economic' factors.

Economically, an item is a candidate for in-house production if the firm has sufficient capacity and if the component's value is sufficient to cover all the variable costs that go into it as well as make some contribution to fixed costs. The variable cost of production is usually less than the purchase cost because its purchase price includes a profit for the supplier (and other members of the marketing channels). Fixed costs of production include plant and equipment investment plus setup and overhead charges.

Low volumes of production tend to favor buying, whereas high volumes favor making. This is because the cost to buy involves little or no fixed component, even though the slope of the total-cost line (that is, the purchase price per unit) is steeper than for the cost-to-make situation. After sufficient volume is produced to cover the fixed cost of making, then it is more profitable to produce the product in-house.

Uncertainties of supply, demand, or product quality complicate the make versus buy decision. However, if historical or market information is available, it may sometimes be converted into a probabilistic form which can be used to reach a better decision.

Strategic Considerations in Make or Buy Decisions

The relevant considerations in make or buy decisions are the same as those of all other purchasing decisions. The strategic considerations are as follows:

- ❖ ***Quality considerations:*** Compare the quality of the purchased item and the quality that the company could have achieved, had it made on its own. If there is no possibility of very wide variation, quality considerations do not weigh heavily in reaching make or buy decisions.
- ❖ ***Quantity considerations.*** Quantity is related to time element, the correct quantity at a given time may not be valid at another time under changed circumstances. Normally, make decision is taken when the supplies are likely to be too small to entrust an outsider. However, it should be considered whether the order can be made big enough to induce outsiders to meet the production needs.
- ❖ ***Cost considerations:*** Cost has relevance in make or buy decisions, when all other decisions are equal or else reasonable cost estimate of the variations should be included to make up an inequality. When making a product, the cost is low buy decision can be given up.

- ***Service considerations (Assured or timely supply):*** The guarantee of supply is an important service consideration. It can be said that supply is more assured when a company makes an item than when it buys.
- ***Competence of know-how required:*** At any time, a firm wanting to produce an item can acquire the necessary potentialities of making the item. But the feasibility of such item depends on cost, which will have to be incurred in acquiring such competence versus buying cost of the same item.
- ***The age of the firm:*** The firm going for make decision must view its decision from its own age point of view. If it is a new industry, it can purchase items. If it is an established firm, it can go for making it.
- ***Tax considerations:*** If the items are purchased outside, thereby no tax is levied, it is advantageous. On the other hand, if an item is manufactured by the company, the availability of tax concession can decide it.
- ***Labour union compulsions:*** Sometimes, labour unions may be against a decision, which they may fear might go against their interest. Generally, making rather than buying items may enable a firm to give more assured and regular employment to its employees.
- ***Sub-contracting:*** Subcontracting is a practice wherein the producer hires the services of another producer to perform some of the manufacturing process. Subcontracting may avoid new investment and the setting up of new plant and equipment on the part of the buyer. Subcontract has the following advantages:
  - *(a)* It is the fastest method of increasing the output;
  - *(b)* The subcontractor uses all the facilities and succeeds in utilizing the capacity so far not being utilized;
  - *(c)* It helps in avoidance of over expansion of productive facilities;

(*d*) It helps in saving time because of skill, experience, and technical know how of workmen;

(*e*) During the times of emergency, when there is need to increase production, subcontracting is ideal.

Economic Factors Influencing Make *versus* Buy Decisions

Inputs

- ❖ Availability of funds and skilled personnel
- ❖ Availability and volume of supply from others
- ❖ Desire for alternative sources of supply

Processing

- ❖ Employee preferences and stability concerns
- ❖ Desire to develop R&D facilities
- ❖ Need to control trade secrets
- ❖ Desire to expand into new product line
- ❖ Need to control delivery lead times
- ❖ Impact upon production flexibility

Outputs

- ❖ Need to control quality or reliability
- ❖ Goodwill and reciprocity impact on customers

Self-learning Activity

Try to answer the following questions on your own.

1. What are the features of vendor rating?
2. What do you mean by price rating scale?
3. Explain buyer-seller relations?
4. Discuss about supplier performance ratings?
5. Write short notes on: make or buy decision.

Summary

- In big organizations, materials are purchased through number of suppliers who are called as vendors.

- Before choosing a vendor, he has to be evaluated about his efficiency by means of certain indicators relating to timely supply, quality, financial conditions, etc.
- Organizations prepare check-list for choosing the vendors and based on the check-list, the vendors are selected.
- To make the purchasing system effective, organizations have to go step-by-step purchasing system. The first step is the pre-purchasing system, the second step is ordering system, and the third system is post-purchasing system.
- In big organization, some of the materials, spare parts, or needed parts can be manufactured by the same organization, which is called as make decision.
- In certain organizations, parts or components needed can be purchased in the open market. Such decision is called as buy decision.
- Whether an organization has to go for make decision or buy decision, depends on the factors like size, technology, financial condition, labour relations, etc.

Quality Considerations in Purchasing

Essentials of Successful Purchasing

Successful purchasing has certain essential elements, which are noted below. Ultimately, these successful elements must lead to quality in purchasing and quality of materials. Following are the essentials of successful purchasing.

- *What to Purchase:* To determine what to purchase is the first essential of successful purchasing. Only to correct material should be procured which has been indented by the authority. This requires giving full specifications and details.
- *From Where to Purchase* Section of right supplier is essential. The order should be placed only to a reliable supplier with whom all conditions have been fully settled.
- *When to Purchase:* The material should be purchased sufficiently in advance so that work does not suffer due to shortage of stores. As far as possible rush purchases should be avoided and materials should be purchased when market rates are low.
- *How Much to Purchase:* It should be according to the amount required by the indentor.
- *At What Rate to Purchase:* Order has to be placed with the lowest but favorable bidder and also where the conditions of payment and discount or commission are most favourable.

- *Maintenance of Purchase Records:* To maintain complete and up-to-date purchase records efficiently is essential. It is also useful in case of any dispute arising with the supplier.

Centralized Vs Decentralized Purchasing

We have already discussed the centralized versus decentralized purchasing in brief in the introduction chapter. It is repeated here in order to bring out the quality considerations in purchasing materials.

Advantages of Centralized Purchasing

- Consistency in buying policies because all purchasing decisions are taken by one department.
- Economy in buying due to better bargaining on price and better terms and conditions with vendors, reduction in transport cost, etc on account of large-scale purchasing.
- Uniformity in purchase records since only one-department handles all the requirements of the organization.
- Economy in maintenance of records in the purchase, receiving, and inspection departments.
- Low inventory investment.
- Reduction in handling and storage costs due to centralization of receiving, inspection, and storage.
- Performance of specialist functions by non-specialists, which will reduce the cost of operations.

Advantages of Decentralized Purchasing

Decentralized purchasing refers to the system of procurement of different divisions or different plants by themselves.

- *Greater flexibility:* Decentralization enables individual buyers to react rapidly to changes in requirements to the divisions to which they are attached.

- ❖ ***Close liaison:*** Since local buyers are in close contact with their respective divisions, they can render greater assistance to them by providing information on probable price, delivery schedule, etc to the department concerned.
- ❖ ***Accountability:*** A local buyer under the decentralized system is under the control of a senior executive of the division and the executive can be held responsible for production lost due to the failure attributable the buyer.

Both centralized and decentralized purchasing have their own merits and demerits. The most common concept is to have a combination in which both centralized and decentralized purchasing can be followed. The merits of such principle is as follows:

- ❖ ***Companies with one manufacturing division:*** Here, all buying activities can be carried out by one department.
- ❖ ***Companies with different manufacturing divisions:*** Each division to have its own buyer to coordinate the activities of the division and all buyers in turn to be responsible to the chief purchasing executive.
- ❖ ***Companies with widely spread over plants owning a group of companies:*** The combination of centralized and decentralized concepts work better in such situations. Each plant or division may have separate purchasing department under the control of head of the division with a centralized purchasing agency:
  - *(a)* to coordinate the activities and directing the policies of the local buyers; and
  - *(b)* to undertake contract buying of important materials.

Value Analysis

According to Dean S. Ammer, "Value Analysis is the study of the relationship of design, function, and cost of any product, material or service with the object of reducing its cost through modification of design or material specification, manufacture by a more efficient process, change in source of supply (external or internal), or possible elimination or incorporation into a related item. Value analysis (VA) is one of the most important techniques of inventory management for reducing costs. It involves application of wide variety of skills for the purpose of achieving a reduction in cost and improvement in quality. It is an organized, creative and profit oriented approach for identifying and avoiding unnecessary costs. The knowledge of value function and cost factor serves to control cost and wastage. Lawrence D. Miles was responsible for developing this technique and naming it. In recent years it also been known as 'molecular engineering' or 'vertical thinking'.

$$\text{Value} = \frac{\text{Function}}{\text{Cost}} \quad \text{or} \quad \frac{\text{Worth}}{\text{Price}}$$

Value analysis is further defined as "an organized creative approach which has, as its objective, the efficient identification of unnecessary cost-which provides neither quality nor use nor life nor appearance nor customer features". Many organizations find that putting value analysis into practice, the act of implementation, is often slow and ineffective despite the best intentions of everyone involved. The problems of implementation are psychological as well as mechanical. But if the full advantages of value analysis are to be exploited, this is the area where new thinking is needed. There is a strong case for value analyzing value analysis.

Value analysis is an organized creative approach, which has for its purpose the efficient identification of unnecessary costs, i.e. costs that provide neither quality nor use nor life nor appearance nor customer features. It is a multisided methodology to enhance the product value by improving the relationships of worth to cost through a study of the function of the product. It focuses the attention of various departments, such as design, production, marketing, industrial engineering and materials, on the objective of getting the best value for the money spent, and at the same time ensuring equivalent performances.

Value analysis embodies the main six basic Principles, viz., functional analysis, value thinking, systematic method, organized group work, integrated product planning and rationalization, and accelerated completion. In functional analysis, the function of the product is detached from its design and form. After this detachment, and with the help of functional thinking, isolated from the product, many alternatives for solving the prescribed function fulfillment may be devised and those which are the most valuable and which best perform the function may be followed up.

Types of Values

Values can be of different types as per the demand for it. Generally values are classified as given below.

- ***Use of Functional Value:*** The properties and qualities, which accomplish a use, work of service or purposes.
- ***Esteem Value:*** The properties, features or attractiveness, which cause us to want to own it.
- ***Cost Value:*** The sum of labour, material and various other costs required to produce it.
- ***Exchange Value:*** Properties or qualities, which enable us to exchange it for something else, we want for example money.
- ***Time Value:*** The property of the goods or services rendered at the right time of need.
- ***Place Value:*** The quality of the goods, which increases the utility by virtue of its location.
- ***Value based on overall or ultimate objectives:*** This may include benefits to organization, industry or community.

Based on these classifications, value is defined as "the minimum money, which has to be expended in purchasing or manufacturing a product to create the appropriate use of esteem factors". In fact, the heart of value analysis techniques is the functional approach. It relates cost of the product to the function.

Benefits of Value Analysis

- Value analysis applies to everything because everything has a function to perform.
- Value analysis is a function-oriented study compared to item-oriented study for conventional methods.
- Value analysis helps in identifying unnecessary costs for their subsequent elimination for improved value.
- Value analysis is a team approach with its members drawn from various disciplines connected with the job.
- Value analysis plays an important role in human resource development to create a company culture.

Tools of Value Analysis

There are two tools available for value analysis:

A. Design Analysis

Design analysis can be used to greatest advantage under the following conditions. Design analysis is predicated on the assumption that material specifications can be changed. Therefore, the first condition of application requires that a firm's material specifications not be tied down rigidly be its products or processes. The greater the flexibility in the specifications, the greater is the potential value of this technique.

- A design analysis programme can be most easily supported when a firm produces, on a recurring basis, a large number of different products. Further, the probability of finding untapped cost reduction areas is greater when each of these products is made up of a large number of complex components.
- Greatest benefits accrue when a material is used in large quantities, either by virtue of a high rate of usage in one product or a lesser rate of usage in each of several products.
- The opportunity to effect significant changes is greater when product designs have not been highly refined by

similar analyses during earlier stages of developments. Thus if specifications are originally developed by the use of extensive interdepartmental participation, opportunities to produce savings through subsequent design analysis are reduced. Conversely, when a product design is modified frequently, opportunities for savings usually increase.

- From the value analyst's point of view, a nonstandard industrial item presents more lucrative possibilities for design change than does a standard item whose design has been refined by its manufacturer.
- The technique is most applicable to a product on which a single design change can be effected without altering the performance of a large number of other components of the product. In general, this favors mechanical designs as opposed to some electrical and thermodynamic designs in which all parts of the product are intricately interrelated.
- The chance for profitable design change on a given product increases as the availability of alternative production materials increases.

B. Cost Analysis

When strong price competition exists among suppliers, competitive forces tend to keep prices in line with costs. Under these conditions, most suppliers have value-analyzed their own products, and cost analysis by the purchaser usually uncovers very few high-cost components. The buyer therefore finds cost analysis most effective when dealing with nonstandard materials or with standard materials whose markets do not exhibit rigid price structures. Likewise, greatest benefits accrue to the buyer when dealing in large quantities of materials.

Gage's Twelve Steps for Value Analysis

In the carrying out of a VA exercise, twelve steps have been identified by Gage. They are as follows:

1. Select the product to be analyzed

Here the problem is to identify the product, which will give the greatest return for the costs incurred in the analysis itself. Rules are obviously impossible to lay down but the following indicate situations likely to produce worthwhile results:

- A multiplicity of components
- A large forecast usage
- A small difference between use value and cost value
- Considerable market competition
- A long-designed product.

2. Extract the cost of the product

The cost required here is the marginal or out-of-pocket cost. An absorption cost would involve decisions on the proportioning of overheads, which could easily distort any apparent cost savings. The calculation of marginal cost is not always easy, and it is here that companies first experience difficulties in value analysis. At this stage details of individual components are not required.

3. Record the number of components

In general, the larger the number of parts the greater the chance of cost-reduction.

4. Record all the functions

This forces consideration of the purpose of the product. Many products serve more than one purpose and all the functions should be stated here, preferably in verb-noun form.

5. Record the number required currently, and in the foreseeable future

This gives magnitude to the effort, which can be expended, and the costs incurred in the analysis.

These five questions are fact-finding' — they firmly establish the bases upon which all further work is created.

6. Determine the primary function

While a number of functions may be present simultaneously, it is not possible to consider them all at the same time-some order of priority must be established. This is done by reconsidering the list prepared in step 4 and deciding which would be the primary function according to the purchaser/user of the product.

7. List all other ways of achieving the primary function

It is here that value analysis requires the presence of a number of people, the value analysis team. Ideas are obtained by means of a 'creativity' of 'brainstorming' session at which ideas are generated and advanced by means of a free flow of ideas. It involves a relaxed atmosphere with an absence of criticism and a desire to contribute something by all present. The purpose of the leader is to stimulate these contributions and to create the freedom of thought and behavior, which are essential. Judgments on ideas are withheld until a later date—the more outrageous the idea, the more welcome it should be both for itself and as a stimulant.

8. Assign costs to all the alternatives

To avoid losing the momentum of the brainstorming session, costs must be assigned to the various alternatives as rapidly as possible, but it is better not to try to assign these costs during brainstorming or the free flow of ideas will be dammed. It is probably desirable to adjourn the VA meeting and reconvene it later when the costs are available. To avoid too much delay 'order of magnitude' costs are acceptable.

9. Examine the three cheapest alternatives

Steps 7 and 8 allow the three cheapest alternatives to be selected and examined for feasibility and performance. The design of the new product will begin to emerge at this stage.

10. Decide which idea should be developed further

From step 9 and the examination carried out there, a decision is taken upon which idea should be developed further.

11. See what other functions need to be incorporated

Re-examination of step 4 will show which other functions have not already been incorporated in the suggestions in step 10. While the 'new' product is being developed, the value analysis committee can undertake the final step.

12. Ensure that the new product is accepted

Conservatism, the principle of 'worry-minimization' and sheer inertia will all combine to resist new ideas. To forestall this, the VA team should consider the ways in which the new idea can be 'sold'. This will almost certainly require.

- A model
- Anticipated savings
- Anticipated capital expenditure
- Improvements in value and a proposed plan in terms of
- Critical Path Analysis network.

Conditions, Which Make the Technique More Effective

Value analysis is a scientific and creative approach. Its focus starts from purchasing function to customer relationship management in an organization. A team representing all departments and heading by a separate professional is essential for value analysis. Further the following conditions make the technique more effective.

1. Type of Product

Value Analysis offers the greatest potential savings where the products are multi-component assemblies and therefore it is more adaptable to the engineering industry than to process industries such as chemicals or food.

2. Volume of Production

Annual savings from Value Analysis are greatest where production is on a large scale. Minor improvements can be suggested much more frequently than major improvements and these will only be worthwhile where volume of output is high. It must be remembered that even in cases of large products such as turbines, ships and buildings, large quantities of many simple items are used, such as screws, rivets, piping and cables that provide mass production saving opportunities. Further more, large items are likely to yield the greatest unit savings point of view, the disadvantages of small quantity production.

3. Variety of Product

The effectiveness of Value Analysis increases with the variety of products of parts. The greater the range of items with which the design staff is concerned, the less attention they can ay to each item, and the greater is the likelihood of alternative designs and materials being overlooked by them. In addition, variety offers greater scopes for inter product standardization of parts example F.H.P. Motors switchgears.

4. Type of Market

Principally companies engaged in price competition in a consumer market have exploited value analysis. Where the eye-appeal of the product is a vital selling factor, however, there could be some restriction in the scope for savings.

Companies whose products sell particularly through technical competence, such as makers of precision instruments and scientific equipment, may appear to have less need considering their detailed costs. Further more, design staff are much more likely to look upon a cost reduction drive as an attack on quality and their resistance may be considerable, particularly where a high proportion of the parts are bought-out.

5. Liaison with Suppliers

Where outside suppliers of materials and parts are of a type which because of the nature of their product are responsive to design and specification changes, then further hope is provided for value analysis through suggestions both from and such suppliers.

From suppliers, in that one can view their technical expertise in a specialized field and their knowledge of cost savings solutions to similar problem elsewhere.

To suppliers, in that value analysis team can assist the supplier use the technique to reduce his costs sharing the resulting benefit as agreed. Cooperating on these lines is most likely in the engineering and allied industries serving a consumer market.

Self-learning Activity

Try to answer the following questions on your own.

1. What are the essentials of successful purchasing?
2. What is value analysis?
3. Cost analysis as a tool of value analysis—comment?

Summary

- While purchasing the materials, quality should be one of the considerations to be followed by the materials manager.
- To maintain quality, the essential elements of purchasing like what to purchase, where to purchase, when to purchase, and price of purchasing, etc must be followed by the materials department.
- In maintaining the quality, centralized purchasing has certain merits like uniformity in purchasing, maintaining quality controls, cost reduction steps, etc.
- In maintaining the quality, decentralized purchasing has also merits like decentralized decisions, accountability by managers, etc.
- Value analysis is an important tool through which the quality of materials is maintained.
- The major objective of value analysis is to identify an unnecessary cost involved in materials eliminate the unnecessary costs to improve the value of materials.

Purchasing Systems 5

Purchasing Systems

Forward Buying

Forward buying is nothing but committing an organization into the future. The buyer commits to buy at a future date a contacted quality at a concentrated price, whatever may be the ruling market price then. The trader makes such moves with a speculative interest with an idea that the actual prices will rise in the future and hence he will be able to make profits. The reasons for the industrial buyer are different. He seeks to protect his organization from any future shortages or undue increases in price. He is interested in having an uninterrupted supply of materials.

Hedging

Hedging is slightly different from more forward buying. In this case the buyer tries to protect himself in the future by entering into two transactions—a purchase and a sale in two markets whose prices move up and down together. Thus the profit or loss sustained in the buying transaction is compensated by the loss or profit in the selling transaction.

Stockless Purchasing

Here the items, that are required in large quantities and for which the seller has other markets as well can consider them for stockless or zero stock buying. The seller holds the stocks in a convenient location so that the buyer can draw from it according to his needs.

Under this system the financial responsibility for the inventory is that of the seller. The goods may be held at the buyer's premises or at the seller's premises. If this system is to succeed then the buyer and seller must have very sound relations and source selection has to be done very carefully. As the seller performs the additional service of holding inventory, the prices may be slightly higher. But this increase in price is compensated by the decrease in carryi8ng cost for the buyer.

Blanket Orders

Blanket orders are generally entered into for low valued and 'C' class items. The main consideration is that the system should be so designed as not to increase the cost of the item significantly due to ordering.

Blanket orders are usually entered into for a period of one year. The time limits can vary. The price can be agreed on or can be the prevailing market price when the supply is effected. In such cases more are established for deciding the market price and there can be upper and lower limits. Being a blanket order the items may be indicated individually or can be generally categorized. The major advantage of a blanket order is that the entire routine of purchasing is not gone through for a minor low value item and the item thus gained can be gainfully used elsewhere for procuring high value items.

System Contract

In system contracting the seller effectively becomes the material lanner for the buyer. It is a long-term contract between the buyer and the seller and provides for the automatic replenishment of the consuming departments stocks by the seller. The consumer sets his requisition supplied directly from the approved vendor. The ordering procedure is simplified thus leading to a reduction of paper work. The system is designed to assist both the buyer and the seller. Regularly consumed low value items are usually system contracted.

Rate and Running Contracts

The principle of rate and running contract is for a centralized agency to enter into a contract with suppliers on the rates applicable to supply of materials for a particular period of time. In rate contracts only the rate is fixed while in running contracts the quantities with variation allowances are also fixed. The centralized agency gets information from its various constituents about the different needs, consolidates these needs and then enters into a contract with probable suppliers.

Cash Purchases

A major reason for such purchases is that these items are required urgently and are such values that would not cause any harm to the organization even if the prices paid are on the higher side. Theoretically such an approach is very valid especially if all the occasionally needed minor items are grouped together and purchases on a single visit to the bazaar whereby reducing the ordering cost to negligible amounts.

Tenders

The prime objective of buying through tenders is to avoid any nepotism and undue favor. Buying should be as impersonal as possible and should foster a spirit of competition so that the prices quoted in the tenders are most competitive. This system is usually adopted by government agencies because not only have they to choose the best supplier but must also show that they are chosen without any bias. Private sector organizations usually adopt this method for the purchase of items whose values are high. A major disadvantage of tender buying is that the minimum administrative lead-time for order placing will be two months.

Sub-contracting

One of the most commonly used systems for procuring manufactured components and sub-assemblies is to sub-contract the manufacture of these items to properly chosen resources. The decision to sub-contract is based on factors such as capacity utilization, cost of manufacture better opportunities for existing facilities and availability of technology. The major advantages of sub-contracting are that the sub-contractor is a specialist in the line, usually has a smaller establishment and hence lower overheads and is able to provide the services at a cheaper rate than the actual manufacturing would cost the buying organization.

Practice of Reciprocity

Purchasing executives have often to contend with the situation of reciprocal buying where they are forced to buy their requirements from the customers of their organization. There can be no harm in reciprocal buying so long as the other factors such as quality, price, delivery and schedule are even.

Purchase Timing

The purchasing executive must make a fundamental policy decision concerning the timing of purchases fro certain major materials. Basically, he can choose one of the two alternatives:

(i) Purchase according to current requirements;

(ii) Purchase according to market conditions.

If he adopts the first policy, he bases his purchasing schedule strictly on the volume of his firm's current needs, and largely disregards the action of the market in which the purchase is made. If the manager adopts the second policy in addition to considering anticipated needs, he bases purchase-timing decisions, in part, on the action of the market. In this case he may engage in three types of buying activity:

(i) Speculative buying;

(ii) Forward buying;

(iii) Hand-to-mouth buying.

Speculative Buying

A speculator buys an item at one price with the intention of profiting on the transaction by selling it at a higher price.

A speculator adds no value to the purchased item, and provides no service to customers, beyond that intrinsic in supplying the item itself. This type of purchasing activity has not place in the normal functions of an industrial purchasing department. If a firm wishes to engage in this type of speculation, such activity should be organized and administered apart from the normal.

A second type of speculative buying is conducted by some purchasing department, and many authorities argue that it is a legitimate function of the purchasing office. This type of buying involves the purchase of material in excess of foreseeable requirements, in anticipation that a need will arise for the material and that the firm will profit by making the purchase at the current price. Opportunities for purchase of this kind arise when a market drops temporarily and the buying firm has sufficient working capital to finance the speculative investment.

Forward Buying

Forward buying is the practice of buying materials in a quantity exceeding current requirements but not beyond actual foreseeable requirements. The distinction between speculative buying and forward buying is that in the latter case, a definite production need for the material exists, while the former case it does not.

There are three major objectives which justify a policy of forward buying:

(a) A significant portion of the forward buying done in unstable markets is designed to take advantage of what the buyer believes to be favourable price situation. He merely attempts to fulfill his known needs at the "best price". Forward buying may also permit a buyer to purchase in quantities sufficiently large to receive volume freight rates, which reduce unit costs;

(b) Occasionally, when a material is purchased in an unstable market, the purchasing firm may find it advantageous to know material and production costs before beginning manufacturing operations in which the material will be used. Such would be the case when the finished gods are sold under a contract involving a predetermined price;

(c) Forward buying reduces the risk of inadequate delivery in the event of an impending material shortage, possible transportation difficulties or the possibility of unreliable performance by a supplier.

Hand-to-mouth Buying

Hand-to-mouth buying is the practice of buying material to satisfy current operating requirement in quantities smaller than those normally considered economical. As the term indicates, the production operation literally exists on a hand-to-mouth supply of materials.

In the case of some high-value materials, it is difficult indeed to draw the line between a hand-to-mouth purchase and a purchase made to satisfy current operating requirement. A hand-to-mouth purchase can be defined as one which provides operating coverage from a bare minimum up to approximately three or four weeks.

There are three basic reasons for pursuing a hand-to-mouth buying policy:

(a) If material is purchased in an unstable market, hand-to-mouth buying saves money when prices are dropping, because the buyer does not accumulate a high-priced inventory. It loses money when the market is rising. But when conducting over the duration of the entire price cycle, hand-to-mouth buying permits purchasers to buy their total requirement at approximately the average market price for the cycle.

(b) In the event that a firm plans an engineering design change, which renders some materials obsolete, hand-to-mouth buying prevents inventory losses.

Occasionally, firms require additional cash for operating purpose; they may also be forced to reduce the indirect expenses of carrying inventory These demands can be temporarily satisfied by reducing inventories and using hand-to-mouth buying.

Stores Management

Meaning and Significance of Store-keeping

Store-keeping is a servicing facility, inside an organization, responsible for proper storage of the material and then issuing it to respective departments on proper requisition. The custodian of stores is generally known as storekeeper or Store-controller. Those items, which are not in use for some specific duration e.g. spare parts and the raw materials, are called as stores and the building or space where these are kept is known as storeroom. Alford and Beauty say that, "store-keeping is that aspect of material control which is concerned with the physical storage of goods. In the words of Maynard, the duties of store-keeping are to receive materials to protect them while in storage from damage and unauthorized removal, to issue the materials in the light quantities, at the right time, to the right place and to provide these services promptly and at least cost".

Stores are generally located in ill-equipped and badly and poorly ventilated buildings. The executives of stores management are generally paid less in comparison to executives of other departments. These factors are responsible for mismanagement of stores resulting in discrepancies in issue of material, loss of items in stock, mistakes in vouchers etc. All these results in undue delay in production.

It is an established fact that more than 70 per cent of the capital of an enterprise is invested in stores. Thus, for efficient and economic utilization of capital the importance of stores cannot be ignored. The management of stores should be entrusted to experience, sincere and efficient personnel and the location of stores should be at some proper and sift place.

Stores System

Well-designed stores system and procedure ensure timely information for decision-making. Function of Stores starts even before material moves in the inventory" Stores System can be broadly classified in two categories: *(i)* close; and *(ii)* open.

Stores System	
Closed	**Open**
1. All materials are stored in a closed/controlled area 2. No other person than the stores personnel is permitted in the area 3. Materials can leave or enter the storage area only by authorized documents. 4. Maximum physical security. 5. Tight accounting control of inventory material.	1. There is no specific storage closed/ controlled area. Stores are maintained in suitable/convenient locations. 2. Every individual has access to any storage facility. 3. After the receipt of the material it is delivered to respective department to expedite the production activity. 4. Chances of pilferage high. 5. Less emphasis on accounting control of the material.

Function of Stores

The term 'storage' deals with pre-production and in-process holding of inventories and supplies awaiting use in the manufacturing operations, while, 'warehousing' implies the holding of finished goods (and in some cases disposable inventory) awaiting shipment. J.M. Apple states the storage functions as follows:

- The determination of what items to store;
- The quantity to store;

- The amount of space required
- Control of the overall activity; and
- A system for co-coordinating the operations and facilities.

Store-keeping is the function of receiving, storing and issuing of inventories. In almost all industrial units, the inventories represent a very large investment. It is, therefore, important that strict orderliness and methods are employed to ensure accuracy, preservation and safety at all stages of inventory movement and custody. In general the functions and responsibilities of stores can be classified as follows:

- To receive, check and a range all incoming materials and supplies.
- To keep inventories as low as possible consistent with the market conditions.
- To meet the demands of consuming departments by proper issues against authorized requisitions, and account for the consumption.
- To forecast market conditions of the supply an availability of various items.
- To minimize obsolescence, surplus and scrap through proper codification, preservation and handling.
- To highlight stock accumulation, discrepancies and abnormal consumption and effect control measures.
- To maintain accurate records.
- To ensure good store keeping so that inventory handling, materials preservation, stocking, receipt and issue can be done adequately.
- To assist in verification and provide supporting information for effective purchase action.
- To ensure that various documents and reports relating to storage functions are sent to required departments without delay.

Duties of a Store Keeper

The store is part of the material control department, and that the duties of the storekeepers are:

- Receiving and storing in good order and condition all goods including raw materials, purchased parts and components, and partly manufactured items. This may involve a routine handling of material. Special regulations are in force governing the storage of certain chemicals, spirits, and cellulose points, and detailed information on this topic should be obtained from the local factory inspector.
- Issuing goods against authorized requisitions only. The storekeeper should never issue material (except for such items as have been declared 'free issue') without a requisition signed by duly authorized person. A promise by a caller at stores to bring a requisition along later should be disregarded; the storekeeper must regard himself as a cashier in a bank, and should not honor a cheque unless it is presented and signed.
- Marshalling goods against sets of documents. It is frequently convenient for the storekeeper to assemble together all the materials required for a particular works order. This material can then either be issued against a summarized material requisition or against a single pack containing all the individual documents. Stores are often provided with special 'job' trolleys on which the marshaled goods are placed for subsequent issue.
- Maintaining such records as may be required of him.
- Carrying out any physical stocktaking as necessary.

Layout and Location of Stores

Stores play important role in the running of the factory. Location and layout of the stores should facilitate the production process. However, rarely materials manager is consulted in the matter of layout and location of stores. The very purpose of scientific storage is safety, cost reduction and easy flow of goods. Hence, the following criteria for a good layout are more important in a store than elsewhere:

- The floor loading must be adequate for the most adverse conditions.
- Stores require being secured; that is, they should not be capable of being entered by other than stores' staff.
- Weather roofing must be particularly good-in a production area a leaking roof is immediately observable while in a stores it may be so obscured that considerable damage might be done before it is discovered.
- Special equipment-hoists, lifts, power saws, power guillotines-may need to be shared with other departments.
- Stores racking will prevent normal movement of air, and temperature distribution can be seriously affected.
- Gangways need to be wide enough to take any stores trolleys and fork-life trucks and must allow articles to be withdrawn from bins and racks, but in general it is not necessary for them to be as wide as production gangways.
- Items used most frequently should be located nearest the issuing windows.
- Heavy or bulky items should be stored as low as possible, although the use of truck hoists can allow heavy items to be lifted to heights of 20 feet and over.
- Shelves and bins should not be so deep as to prevent easy access to the back.
- A receiving area, where goods can be separated and unpacked prior to dispersal, should be provided.
- An assembly area where all the parts for a particular job can be assembled before being issued is useful.
- Computing scales, which should be used wherever possible, must be screened from draughts.
- A location system enabling the position of any single item to be pin-pointed is essential. A simple system is to give a letter reference to each line of bins, and number the bins in each line serially from one end. This reference

should be shown on the stock record card, but in addition a location index should be provided in stores.

- Storing is essentially a volumetric problem, that is, it depends on height as well as floor area. Use of height can be increased by employing some of the modern fork trucks in conjunction with pallets.

Stock Verification

It is the process of physically measuring or weighting the entire range of items in the stores and recording the results in a systematic manner. The purposes served by stock verification are as follows:

- To reconcile the stock records and documents for their accuracy and usefulness;
- To identify areas, which requires more disciplined document control;
- To back up the balance sheet stock figures;
- To minimize the pilferage and fraudulent practices. Stock verification is usually carried out by the materials audit department, reporting to either the materials manager or the internal audit. One person is usually given the exclusive responsibility with adequate facilities and authority. Physical verification can be carried out periodically of on continuous basis.

Periodic Verification

Under this system, the entire cross section is verified at the end of one period, which is usually the accounting period. In big organizations this is not achieved in a day and usually several days are taken to complete this task. As no transactions can take place during the verification, this task. As no transactions can take place during the verification this could pose some problems Physical verification requires. Careful planning and exception. The various steps involved are detailed below:

A detailed programme should be checked out giving complete breakdown of the process store wise and item wise. This should be done in consultation with the material management and finance departments. Necessary stock verification cards and check sheets must have clear cut instructions on their jobs and schedule for proper accountability. During the verification process all transaction must be stopped. In other words, should not be any receipts or issues. All stock verification cards should be serially numbered for easy reference and control. Separate provisions must be made available for items which are damaged or deteriorated. Selected areas and items must be allocated to each stock taking person so that orderly completion of the job without duplication or omission is ensured. It will be necessary to separately verify items, which are under inspection items sent out to supplies for processing and stocks at various stockyards.

SPECIMEN OF VERIFICATION SHEET

Stock location .... Serial No ....

Part Number .... Date ....

Part Description ....

Unit of Quantity No/Materials/ Kgs/Litres

Rate .... Quantity on hand ....

Value of Stock on hand ....

Audited by s/d

Checked by s/d

Remarks

Damaged Deteriorated Others

Such sheets as shown a head are prepared for each item and values are worked out for different classifications. The total of such values gives the value of the stock on hand as verified. Then this is tallied against the book figures or stock records. Discrepancies if any one noted down. Minor discrepancies are taken care of by correcting the stock records. Any major discrepancies need further analysis so that causes can be identified and remedied. Any major discrepancies need further analysis so that causes can be identified and remedied. Allowances regarding acceptable margins of tolerances of conversion, weighing and measuring, as well as for evaporation, weighing and measuring, as well as for evaporation, most be clearly laid down. Top management's sanction can then be sought for writing off deficiencies or valuing surplus.

Continuous Verification

Under this system, verification is done through out the year as per a predetermined plan of action. A- Items may be verified thrice a year; B- items twice a year; and C- items once a year. It, therefore, presupposes that a perpetual inventory record for each item is maintained showing all transactions so that reconciliation can be done. The advantages here are:

Work can be independently carried out by materials audit department staff. Investigation with regard to discrepancies are spread over the year and hence detailed analysis is possible. Final accounts are prepared expeditiously if continuous verification is done as per plan. There is no need to freeze the entire operation of the stores as verification is done throughout the year based on perpetual inventory records. Any time stock records are more up to date when compared with the periodic verification system.

Process of Verification

Items are verified by counting in the case of bearings, by weight in the case of sheets, by measuring in the case of lubricants and so on. However, when large stocks of items such as sand scrap or ore fuel need to be verified, it is based only on estimates as the question of stock verification, the stores personnel should be involved, as they intimately know the locations of various items which results in quicker identification of items. For instance, sometimes may be located in many places. By virtue of their experience only stores personnel will be able to locate them. So the material audit people will have to work in close coordination with them. Discrepancies must be discussed with stores so that any omissions may be rectified and then only should they be reported to top management. Major discrepancies may require are- verification. Such discrepancies may be due to pilferage on a large scale, wrong pasting of records and loose documents control. They require careful analysis and immediate corrective measures.

After discrepancies have been noted stock adjustments must be made using standard stock adjustment documents duly signed by the appropriate authority. A typical stock adjustment form is shown below

DISCREPANCY VOUCHER

Date of verification		Serial No	
Part No		Serial No / Ref. No	
Part Description		Stock verification sheet	
Location Code			
Quantity as per record			
Quantity on verification			
Discrepancy	Amount:	Value:	Surplus
Prepared by S/d			Deficient
Approved by S/d			

After the approval, the stock records can be corrected surprise checks and verifications are made by materials audit department to detect any fraudulent acts. Material audit plays the rate of a watch dog of store, pointing out weak areas and remedying them. It assists in accurate records keeping and smooth finalization of annual accounts.

Self-learning Activity

Try to answer the following questions on your own:

1. Write notes on: *(a)* Hedging; *(b)* Blanket Orders?
2. What do you mean by speculative buying?
3. What are the duties of a storekeeper?
4. How is stock verified?

Summary

- There are various purchasing systems available for the materials manager. The application of each purchasing system depends on the financial position of the organization, purchasing policy of the organization, market conditions, etc.
- While purchasing the materials, purchase timing is also equally important. The timing of purchase should match the purpose of purchasing and economy to be maintained in purchasing.
- Stores management is an important activity in materials management. Through proper storing, wastage of materials can be avoided and the inventory position can be monitored properly.
- For effective store keeping, stock taking is very important. Stocks must be verified frequently as per the needs and objectives of the organization.

Materials Handling and Maintenance

Principles and Importance of Materials Handling

In an industrial undertaking, various kinds of equipments are used for different purposes. In general these equipments can be divided into three categories—storage, handling and warehousing.

The term 'inventory handling' and 'materials handling' are used interchangeably. The materials department, being the fountainhead of the movement of materials in the concern, can ill afford to overlook the technological developments in this field. It has to plan its requirements thoroughly and minimize the total movement expenditure, at the same time maintaining the service level.

Definition

Inventory handling is the art and science of moving, packaging, and storing of materials in any form. It covers the whole chain of handling from acquisition of brought-out items up to an including delivery to the customer.

Materials handling includes all movement of materials in a manufacturing situation. The American Materials Handling Society has defined it as follows:

"Materials handling is the art and science involving the movement, packaging, and storing of substances in any form".

Thus, materials handling is that part of mechanization which is concerned with the transporting, positioning and storing of materials in organization.

Importance of Materials Handling

In large number of industries inventory handling is the heart of their manufacturing processes. Inventory handling is more costly than labour and equipment costs. Hidden costs such as ineffective plant utilization, wasted employee time, extended inventory of both goods—in process and raw materials, excess demurrage charges, and product quality must be recognized. This handling procedure affects the size of inventory at various stages to a great extent and thus affects the investment in inventory and the cost of the product.

It is obvious that no value is added to the end-product through materials handling. However, poor materials handling may result in delays leading to idling of equipment. "Nearly 50 per cent of the production cycle time in many industries is spent on handling materials".

According to James Apple, "Items are being worked on only 20 per cent of the time and in storage or undergoing handling 80 per cent of the time, 22 per cent of industries manpower is used in handling materials and throughout industry, 50 tones of product must be handled to produce one ton of finished goods".

Good inventory handling means more production, and it also means more goods for more people at lesser cost. The results of a good inventory handling system are:

- Reduced labour cost at receiving and dispatching points.
- Increased production;
- Reduced cost of transportation;
- Reduced cost of indirect labour;
- Better inventory control;
- Reduced fatigue and physical strain on workers;
- Reduction/elimination of damages at all stages of materials handling;
- Cost reduction throughout resulting in increased output and increased profits;

- Better utilization of floor space;
- Improved labour relations;
- Increased safety—both employees' safety as well as product safety.
- Lowered insurance rates.

According to the Materials Handling Handbook there are 430 kinds of materials handling equipments divided into the following nine major categories: *(i)* Conveyors; *(ii)* Cranes; *(iii)* Positioning, weighting and control equipment; *(iv)* Industrial vehicles; *(v)* Motor vehicles; *(vi)* Rail-road cars; *(vii)* Marine carriers; *(viii)* Aircraft; and *(ix)* Containers and supporters.

Inventory handling may be divided into two groups, namely, manual handling and mechanical handling:

1. Manual operated equipments include hand trucks, platform trucks with side or pellets, fort trucks, etc.
2. Mechanical handling equipments: These may be divided into floor type and overhead type. Further, the equipments may be continuous type for vertical lift as well as horizontal lift, intermittent type like cranes.

Materials handling is the movement of materials from the receiving department through production operations to final shipment. The materials handling system consists of the network of facilities that receive, store, transport, and deliver the materials.

For manufacturing firms, materials include raw materials, work in process, finished goods, and supplies, plus scrap, waste, and other effluent. Materials handling activities for raw materials range from transporting coal in rail cars in Kentucky, to helicopter logging in Oregon, to moving oil through pipelines in Alaska. A variety of materials handling equipment including conveyors, trucks, and transfer machines are used for work in process and finished goods.

Materials handling in a factory costs as much as 20 to 30 per cent of the payroll cost, but it adds no tangible value to the product. Nevertheless, it does much to facilitate production by transporting needed materials to proper locations at the right time. Without a good system, materials are easily lost or damaged, and production is delayed. This is why major firms employ skilled materials handling engineers. They carefully plan the flow of materials, conduct feasibility and cost studies for alternative types of handling equipment, and make recommendations concerning the selection, use, and maintenance of equipment.

Materials Handling Guidelines

- Plan handling as a system;
- Minimize handling volume and frequency;
- Maximize load size and weight;
- Use direct, rapid, steady flows;
- Minimize idle time of equipment and operators;
- Allow for breakdown, changes, and maintenance.

Some basic guidelines to facilitate good materials handling practices are given as follows:

Planning the handling as a system, from the supplier through the process to the consumer, facilitates coordination among the departments of the firm. This improves handling efficiency by providing opportunities to combine some handling and eliminate others.

Both the total amount of handling and the number of times handled should be minimized. In addition, mechanized devices should be used to minimize the human effort required to load and unload the materials handling facilities whenever practical.

Maximizing the load size takes advantages of economies of scale and reduces the total transportation time. The load size must, however, be balanced against desirable levels of work in process.

Using *direct, steady flows* minimizes backtracking, zigzagging, and parallel movement—all of which take up both time and manufacturing space. Unnecessarily long conveyors can also generate undesirable increases in the work-in-process inventory.

Idle time of both equipment and operators is wasteful, and empty or practical loads should be avoided.

Unexpected breakdowns and changes always seem to occur at inopportune times. The reality of these problems should be anticipated.

Handling materials in the main activity in storehouses and stock yards. The American Materials Handling Society has defined materials handling as the art and science involving movement, packaging and storing of materials in any form by means of gravity, manual effort or power actuated machinery. Materials handling planning consider motion, time, place, quantity and space.

Principles of Materials Handling

- Shorten or integrate if not eliminate handling
- Deliver materials closest to the point of use
- Move the man in preference to moving the material
- Make the layout to economic handling
- Select right equipment for right job
- Flow process should be correct to eliminate uneconomical movement

Maintenance of Materials

Maintenance of materials is a significant job of the organization. Special care must be taken by the organization in the area of maintenance of materials.

Objectives of Maintenance

- To keep the factory plants, equipment, raw materials, etc in an optimum working condition;

- To keep the equipment safe and prevent the development of safety hazards;
- To ensure specified accuracy to products and time schedule of delivery to customers;
- To keep the production cycle within the stipulated range;
- To reduce maintenance cost and operating costs as low as possible leading to reduction in overhead charges;
- To help the management in taking decisions on new investment, equipment selection, etc.; and
- Help the implementation of suitable procedure for procurement, storage of materials.

Economic Aspects of Maintenance

Maintenance costs can be classified into directs costs and indirect costs.

Direct Costs

(a) Materials—Stores, spares, consumables, etc.

(b) Labour—Maintenance crew, contract labour, etc.

(c) Depreciation on capital equipment and tools used in maintenance.

(d) Carrying cost of maintenance stores.

(e) Overhead expenses chargeable to maintenance operations.

(f) Direct external costs for repairs, inspection, etc.

Indirect Costs

(a) Loss in production

(b) Financial charges

(c) Overhead expenses chargeable to maintenance operations

(d) Idle time expenses

Advantages of maintenance management

- Reduction in production time
- Less overtime pay for maintenance personnel
- Less number of standby equipments needed

- Less expenditure on repairs
- Greater safety to employees

Requirements for effective maintenance management

- Good supervision and administration of maintenance department
- Proper control of work
- Correct, clear, and detail instructions be given to maintenance crew
- Adequate training to personnel
- Proper maintenance record should be maintained
- Adequate stock of spares should be kept
- Surroundings should be dust free and clean
- Maintenance department should remain in contact with planning and purchase department

Handling of Wastes, Surplus, Scrap and Obsolete Materials

Handling of Wastes

Any material, which does not add value to the product during product cycle, may be termed as waste. Waste may be unavoidable in the production process but can be controlled or reduced.

Classification of Waste

Waste can be classified on the basis of:

- ❖ Resources wasted
- ❖ Origin
- ❖ Property
- ❖ Recoverability

Waste Resources

Material resources like solids, liquids and gases can be wasted. Energy resources like physical, human and solar energy can be wasted. Time resource can be wasted. Capital in the form of capacity, equipment, machine hours and inventory can be wasted. Services like communication, transport, health etc. can be wasted. Life or human resources, data and information may also suffer wastages.

Origin of Waste

It could be industrial, residential, commercial, office, municipal, construction and demolition, agricultural etc. Materials wasted are hazardous or non-hazardous. Wastes can be recovered into some useful resource, material waste recycled. Non-recoverable wastes are lost with time.

Waste exists is myriad forms — non-workable components, excess inventory, machine downtime, re-work, non-conformance, warranties. Any activity that does not add value is a waste. Re-work is the biggest non-value added activity that a company performs. If we reduce the unnecessary activities or eliminate them, costs will come drastically.

Systematic Approach to Waste Reduction

Through proper planning and control waste can be brought under control. In this context the following approach can be followed:

- First of all the total waste in the whole system is to be recognized;
- Then the stages at which waste is generated are identified;
- Then the sub-stages are identified in which above wastes can be put;
- Then waste-reduction programme is implemented at each stage by planning correcting action and eliminating the cause.

Waste Collection System

Wastes affect the environment, the organization, and public health. Waste collection and transporting is the major cost element, and if efficiently handled, may reduce the overall cost of waste management. Waste collection consumes 80 percentage of waste reduction programme.

The following factors govern the waste collection:

- Separate the waste at source;
- Make arrangement to collect it in suitable containers of the right material and right size;
- Depending upon the generation rate of waste, make arrangements to collect waste from time to time;
- Offer incentives to collect waste at source;
- Make suitable arrangements to collect both the organic and inorganic wastes;
- Carry the waste to the salvage industry for reuse.

Recycling of Wastes

The wastes can be recycled/reused. For this purpose, suitable recycling projects are to be created. In recycling, the waste can be used as input to the same process/system. e.g. recycling of foundry scrap. In recycling, the waste can also be used as input to some other process/system e.g. sugarcane bagasse is used to prepare paper. In reuse of waste, we may generate power or by-product e.g. Bio-gas generates electricity/fuel and molasses produces alcohol. In reclamation, the damaged, rejected or undesired outputs are converted by repair or processing. Recovery is a general term to indicate gain of resources from wastes

Waste Disposal System

Waste can be classified by two categories in terms of its disposal.

1. *Salvable waste:* They have the salvage value e.g. scrap rejected goods, surplus and obsolete items.
2. *Non-salvable waste:* They have no salvage value, but need further processing and treatment for disposal.

Handling of Surplus

Industrial surplus is defined as those materials, which are in excess of the reasonable operational requirements of the concern. Surplus is the state of an item when stock is likely to last longer than a reasonable period or when it is no longer required for use.

Surplus stock generally arises on the following occasions:

- When purchases have been made in larger quantities than the usual requirements. However, when inventory control is pursued with diligence, such situation will not generally occur.
- When operations are suddenly curtailed. This applies mostly to production materials, specially, raw materials and components although tools and certain general stored items also may become surplus in this manner.
- When, the materials are rendered useless due to change in materials specifications the original material is, naturally turned surplus.
- When at the turn of materials procurement, on account of some error or miscalculation that has crept in the wrong item has been purchased.
- When a project is completed, some quantities of the items, used for the commissioning of the project are bound to be left out. This is surplus. In this connection, surpluses emanate from three primary sources:
  - *(a)* Scrap and waste
  - *(b)* Surplus, obsolete or damaged stock items.
  - *(c)* Surplus, obsolete or damaged equipment.

(a) Surplus from Scrap and Waste

Wastage, spoilage, empty drums and bags which are not returnable to suppliers, broken and worn-out tools which are beyond repairs, irreparable parts of machinery, turning and borings from machines are all commonly termed as scrap.

A residue or pieces cut of raw materials during the manufacturing process is wastage. Since, not all the materials injected into production processes are converted into finished products, surplus from production process are inevitable and common feature in every concern.

It is highly impossible for any firm to get rid completely of this type of surplus; however effective and intelligent production planning handling of issue from stores and control can contribute to reduce it.

Surplus that is generated from inefficient use of production machinery, carelessness and poor purchasing are spoilage (wastage) of resources. Items spoiled among the course of manufacture or storage are also spoilage. Spoilage may involve loss of machine hours as well as man-hours. Special care should be extended particularly during storage of perish-at-time items so that spoilage is avoided.

(b) Surplus, Obsolete or Damaged Goods (Stocks)

Items, which are degenerated out-of-date-mostly superseded by a better deign and sophisticated technologies are known as obsolete items. It is quite unreasonable to expect sales forecasting and production planning to match exactly in reality. It is a variety, though not absolutely impossible.

In case of over-anticipation, enthusiastic and optimistic sales forecasting, excess materials are found in the stores. Further, continuous sweeping, successive and rapid changes take place with its sky-rocketing pace in the designs and specifications of the materials and components. So the slow moving items are surplus in this fast moving society. As a consequence, obsolete products and their parts constitute a continuing source of surplus materials.

Excessive forward buying as well as planned over-buying are another common and yet profound source of surplus materials. These entail the hazard of surplus from obsolescence, deterioration and errors in stock-taking and record-keeping.

(c) Surplus, Obsolete or Damaged Equipment

All machines and equipment at some point in their life become surplus for two primary reasons-one, they wear out with passage of time and secondly, they become technologically obsolete with the invention of better technology machines. Machines or tools are seldom worn out; they have to be replaced in view of changed circumstances to avail better functioning and efficiency.

Every manager has been at his wit's end and makes haunting efforts to prolong the life of capital equipments as long as possible. But for the fact of the reasons of obsolescence, breakdowns, introduction of new products or new methods of production, replacement of major capital assets even building becomes mandatory.

For the fact that these obsolete equipments or components can be modified to the latest design or sold to the original user of the original design, they prefer but to dispose of them as surplus - even as scrap in some extreme cases.

Handling of Scrap

The following are some of the categories of materials, which come under the term scrap.

1. Wastage

Pieces cut out of raw materials during manufacturing process are called wastage. The wastage is normally included in the quantity issued and is therefore debited to the job. Raw materials should be purchased in economic sizes to keep wastage at the absolute minimum. In certain cases, intelligent handling of issues can reduce wastage from stores.

When operations such as, turnings, borings, drillings, etc., are carried out on metal bars, sheets, components, etc., a certain portion of the metal is removed by such operations. Similarly sawdust and woodcuttings are obtained when wood is cut. Such arising are stored separately and sold as scrap.

2. Spoilage

Items, which are spoiled during the course of manufacture or storage, are called spoilage. Spoilage in manufacture involves loss of machine hours as well as man-hours. Special care should also be taken to avoid spoilage during storage. In both cases of spoilage, Scrap Notes will cover the items.

3. Irreparable parts of equipment

Certain parts of equipment become irreparable after some years. Examples are crankshaft, connecting rods, bearings, etc., of an engine. Replacement is taken from stores on requisitions and the old ones are thrown into the scrap dump and sold by weight.

4. Scrap tools

Some tools wear out after a period and some break during usage. They are written off from stock by scrap note and sold as scrap tools lest they may be exchanged for new ones by someone or the other.

5. Empties

Empty drums, bags, packing case, etc., which are not returnable to suppliers are treated as scrap and sold.

6. Used oil

In many factories, there is arising of used oil as a result of operating machine tools, etc. They are sold as "scrap" often along with the drum.

7. Obsolete items

Obsolete components, which cannot be sold as spares and therefore written off from the financial books, are sold as scrap.

Disposal of Scrap

Disposal of scrap is effected by:

- Inviting offers from time to time.
- Annual contract
- Public auction.

In the first case lists of scrap showing description of the items and approximate quantities available are circulated to interested parties or advertised in the newspapers once in three months or so and disposal will be effected at the highest price obtained. The procedure followed will be similar to the 'Tender System'.

Sale by annual contract is also effected by circulating lists or advertisement in the newspapers showing the approximate quantity expected to be available during the year. In certain companies where the volume of major items is considerable, the contract is awarded to two or three dealers, but in small size firms it may be convenient to give to one dealer. The annual contract has the advantage that the scrap will be automatically removed from time to time; there will be no large accumulation with possible fire hazard and at the same time valuable space in the factory will be saved.

The procedure followed for auction is briefly given below:

- Materials for auction will be properly listed giving lot number, full description of the material, quantity, etc.
- Sale will be effected on 'as is where is' basis.
- Proposals to sell materials by auction will be adequately advertised.
- A representative each from the Stores and Purchase as well as Accounts departments will supervise auction.
- Often a reserve price is fixed for various items and before a bid is accepted. The officers attending the auction must satisfy themselves that the highest bid obtained is the best in the circumstances.
- A statement showing the highest bids obtained will be signed by the officers attending the auction.
- An amount of 10 per cent to 25 per cent of the accepted bid will be taken, as earnest money from the bidders concerned and a receipt for the same will be issued by the Accounts Department. The balance of the money is to be deposited by the bidder within a fixed time limit.
- On production of the cash receipt for the balance amount, delivery order is issued in favour of the bidder to collect the materials within a reasonable time.

Handling of Obsolete Materials

An obsolete item is one, which has been superseded by another item due to change in design, modification or substitution.

Obsolete materials differ from surplus materials as the latter could be consumed in near future; the former is unlikely to be used.

An item is rendered obsolete under following situations:

1. Design changes

Design changes are effected due to:

- satisfy the customer's desire for variety. This reason is especially dominant among textile and other consumer articles;
- overcome manufacturing difficulties to meet the requirements of quality. Such modifications are made on the basis of suggestions and complaints from vendors or feedback from company's own shops; and
- avoid repetitive failures of certain components based on field reports or complaints from company's service engineers, dealers or customers.

The design changes to satisfy reasons given under: (1) and (2) are never effected abruptly since it results in large-scale obsolescence. Closer co-ordination between the design department and sales department is to be maintained to ensure that design changes watched closely. Reason given in (3) is happened due to failure in technology or its implementation.

2. Product simplification is yet another cause for large scale obsolescence

The management at time may decide to delete a particular product because of its poor sale, its lower contribution or both. This leads to obsolescence of raw materials and components used for the deleted products.

3. Cancellation of orders for items manufactured to buyer's specifications

Sometimes buyers may cancel the orders. In such a case the supplier's sales department should make every effort to sell raw materials, and tools to the same buyer or to others.

4. **Capital replacement** of the obsolete equipment generally renders inventory of replacement parts obsolete

Such parts do not have any usage value to the company. Rarely some equipment may be common to other machines in use, while majority become obsolete.

5. **Completion of a project usually leaves lot of obsolete materials, such as:**
   - Uneven rejection in components-shafts, gears, housing etc. of a custom-built product usually leads to obsolete items.
   - Certain quantities of bricks, cement, wire mesh, etc, is usually left unused on the completion of a construction work.

6. **Substitution is yet another reason for the genesis of obsolete items**

This particularly happens when a production process is changed in terms of its material. Such a change may lead to overall change in production process but old materials do become obsolete.

Self-learning Activity

Try to answer the following questions on your own:

1. Define materials handling?
2. What are the guidelines for materials handling?
3. Write about handling of obsolete materials?

Summary

- Materials handling and maintenance of materials can avoid lot of wastes that may arise in organizations.
- Materials handling and materials maintenance must be undertaken on a scientific basis.
- Experienced staff must be made responsible for materials handling and maintenance of materials.

- Wastes arise in factories and they can be classified on the basis of resource wasted, origin of waste, recoverable waste.
- A waste collection system should be introduced systematically, because disposal of waste can provide income to the organization and keep the environment clean.
- Scrap should be properly collected and they must also be disposed off for an income.
- Obsolete materials can be sold in auction, which can produce income to the organization.

Inventory Management

Meaning, Definition, Importance, and Advantages of Inventory Management

Inventory management, in fact, is an integral part of production planning and control which, according to Charles A. Keopke, may be defined as " the co-ordination of a series of functions according to a plan which will economically utilize the plant facilitates and regulate the orderly movement of goods through their entire manufacturing cycle, from the procurement of all materials to the shipping of finished goods at a pre-determined rate". But, the scope of inventory management is not only restricted to the technique of regulating the movement of inventories, and it rather "covers the entire range of functions which affect the flow, conservation, quality and cost of inventories".

According to B.K. Bhar, inventory management is "a system which ensures the provision of the required quantity of inventories of the required quality at the required time with the minimum amount of capital". Bethel says that inventory management is concerned with planning, directing and controlling the kind, amount, location, movement and timing of the various flows of commodities used in and produced by a business enterprise.

P.R. Gokarn feels, "inventory management covers a wider field and deals with all aspects of inventory supply and utilization as well as costs". It is "an organizational concept that localizes or brings together under one organizational component that responsibility for determining the manufacturing requirements, scheduling the manufacturing process and procuring, storing and dispending materials without allowable cost".

In the words of T.S. Teague, "Inventory management establishes the requirements, provides the availability, determines the value and price levels, and controls the flow of inventories from the initial development of the production requirement until the final delivery of the product to the customer".

It can be inferred from the above definitions of inventory management that there are two guiding principles in inventory management. They are:

1. Adequate inventory has to be maintained to avoid stock-out and causing consequent production held-up and customers' dissatisfaction, and
2. Excessive investment in inventory items must be avoided as it increases carrying cost and results in loss of profit.

Inventory Management *Vs.* Materials Management

Generally, inventory management is taken as the synonymous of materials management. But inventory management and materials management differ from each other so far as their fundamental activities are concerned. Inventory management is the management process whereas materials management is a functional process. To make a clear distinction between inventory management and materials management, we can say that inventory management is the process whereby the investment in inventories in stock is regulated by pre-determined limits set in accordance with the inventory policy established by the management. Whereas on the other hand, materials management refers to the process of providing quantity and quality of materials needed in the manufacturing process with an eye on economy in storage, ordering cost, purchase price and working capital.

It is thus apparent that the activities of inventory management includes the determination of limits of inventories to be held, determination of inventory policies, setting out of investment pattern and follow up to examine the working of inventory policy and effecting changes as and when required. On the other hand, materials management comprises functions relating to the procurement of materials as per schedules so that activities of production may work effectively.

In fact, inventory management is a fundamental operational process of management, which makes materials available in time for production without incurring extra cost for carrying out uneconomic inventories. In brief, it can be said that the idea of inventory management brings mind the following two ideas at a time for achieving the objective of cost control and cost reduction:

1. To have all materials of right qualities at right prices when wanted or needed by the production department; and
2. To keep the capital locked up in stock as low as possible without any delay in production.

On the basis of above mentioned facts, it may be said that in the absence of inventory management, the entire functioning of materials management may be rendered inefficient or aimless, because it refers to a management process whereby the investment in the inventories carried in godown is calculated within the pre-determined limits set in accordance with the inventory policy established by the management on the basis of accounting information and scientific techniques.

Essentials of Inventory Management

There are two levels of inventory control—unit control and rupee control. Purchasing and production executives are primarily interested in unit control. Therefore, they are likely to think order and require in terms units instead of rupees. On the other hand, executives responsible for financial planning and control such as treasurers, controllers, and top management think in terms of financial planning and control of inventories. Thus, a good management must meet these two opposing needs:

1. The maintenance of an inventory that is not detrimental financially; and
2. The maintenance of an inventory of sufficient size and diversity for sufficient operations.

In order to strike a balance between the above said opposing needs the inventory management system should be at placing an order at the right time from the right source to acquire the right quantity at the right price and quality. A company cannot achieve these objectives unless there is an efficient inventory management system.

Scientific Inventory Management System

Inventory management is one of the key result areas in an organization. The followings are the pre-requisites for the successful functioning of the inventory management system:

- Proper co-ordination among departments involved in buying, receiving, inspection, storage and accounting;
- Centralized purchasing under the control of competent authority;
- Proper scheduling of inventory requirements;
- Proper classification of materials with codes, materials standardization and simplification;
- The use of standard forms for orders, requisition etc. upon which only properly written instructions are acceptable;
- Properly authorized and independent persons control the operation of a system of internal checks to ensure that all transactions involving inventories and equipments are carried out as per plan;
- The storage of inventories in a well planned manner and their properly designated location subject to adequate safeguards and supervision;

- The operation of a system of stores control and issue for the effective delivery of inventories upon requisition to departments in the right amount at the time when needed;
- Effective operation of a system of perpetual inventory for possibly determining at any times the amount and value of each kind of inventory in stock;
- Fixation of inventory levels;
- Adequate records to control inventories during production and the quantities manufactured for stock;
- Regular report to management of items purchased, issued from stock, inventories balances, obsolete stock, goods returned to vendors and spoiled or defective items, etc.
- Proper handling of inventories; and
- Effective traffic management.

While establishing inventory requirements, in addition to the above every inventory item or class of item must be analyzed periodically to determine:

- Forecasted usage for the next month, quarter or year
- Acquisition lead-time
- Planned usage during lead-time
- Quantity on hand
- Units in order
- Reserves or safety stock requirements, etc.

Advantages of Inventory

In a large manufacturing concern it is always advantageous to order some type of raw-materials and purchased parts in advance and hold them in stock to be used when required to meet the customers orders. The main advantages or purchasing materials well in advance are the following:

- Sometimes in competition with other manufacturers, delivery requirements (dates), are very tight and if orders for raw-materials or parts are placed after receiving customers order it may not be possible to meet the demand and the required delivery date. It is therefore advantageous to hold inventories;

- Buying and producing material in large quantities is profitable as discounts and concessions are available on large quantity purchases. There is reduced cost per item of selling up machines and plant. There is also reduced clerical work and cost for placing orders less frequently;
- A good industry keeps a ready stock of its product for immediate sale. Inventory of raw materials and parts helps to replace these products faster once they are sold and disposed of;
- There can be difficulties in procurement of raw materials and parts due to unexpected strikes, shortages, power breakdown or period of high demands in relation ton supply. In this case inventories may come to rescue;
- Building up a big inventory will be profitable as later on there may be a rise in prices of various items due to various reasons;
- More products can be manufactured rapidly when raw materials or parts are held in stock;
- Inventories reduce the risk of closing down the plant or keeping workers and machines idle.

Types of Inventories

Generally inventories are classified as raw materials, finished parts, work-in-progress, finished goods, tools and supplies. They are as follows

Raw Materials

Raw materials are those basic materials which have undergone no conversion whatsoever since their receipt from the suppliers. They include items like steel, copper, lead tin, cotton rubber, leather, timber, etc. Raw materials in other words, are those basic materials from which the company manufactures components, parts, and products.

Finished Parts

The bought - out - parts or piece parts are called as finished parts. Bought-out-parts are those finished parts, sub-assemblies or assemblies which are purchased from outside suppliers. These include standard parts as well as parts produced by suppliers to buyer's design. Place-parts are those parts which are manufactured at the company's own plant from the basic raw materials.

Work-in-process

It comprises of items or materials in partially completed condition of manufacture. Raw materials become work-in-progress at the end of first operation and remain in what classification until they become parts of finished goods. Work-in-process can be found on the conveyors, tucks, pallets, in and around the machines, and in temporary areas of storage waiting to be worked upon or assembled.

Finished Goods

These are the final products ready to be sold. Products usually leave work-in process classification and enter into the classification of finished goods at the point of final inspection when they are ready for delivery to the customer or to finished goods store. Normally they bear the label like, 'Tested O.K', Inspected O.K., Checked O.K. etc.

Tools

Tools generally comprises of:

1. Standard tools used on machines such as saws, drills, reamers, taps, chasers, milling cutters, hobs, broaches, form tools, inserts etc.
2. Hand tools such as handsaws, chisels, drill gun, hammers, mallets, needles, pliers, punches, spanners, wrenches etc.

Supplies

The materials used in running the plant or in making company's products, which do not themselves go into the product are called as supplies. Supplies, therefore, include:

- Miscellaneous consumable stores such as brooms, cotton waste, cloth waste, toilet paper, cleaning powder, jute twine, etc.
- Welding, soldering and tinning materials such as electrodes, welding rods, solder, shelter, etc.
- Abrasive materials such as emery cloth, emery belts, sand paper, emery graphite etc.
- Brushes, mops and bobs such as artist's brushes, cleaning brushes, paint brushes, etc.
- Empties such as bags, glass bottles, cardboard boxes, drums, jars, tins etc.
- Oils and greases such as kerosene oil, transformer oil, petrol, diesel oil, lubricating and cutting oils.
- General office supplies such as blotters, candles, sealing wax, ink and ink-pads, nibs, pencils and refills, files, pins, clips, carbon paper, stencil paper, erasers etc.
- Printed forms such as envelopes, letter heads, enquiry forms, order acceptance forms, purchase order forms, order amendment forms, goods receipt reports, discrepancy notes, vouches, debit notes, credit notes, invoices, etc.
- Ledgers and journals such as goods inward register, goods receipt register, sales register, sundry creditors register, sundry debtors register, cash book, loan register, sales journal, purchase journal, general ledger etc.
- Electric supplies such as cables, clips, fuses, lamps, lamp holders, hoses, shades, switches etc.
- Machinery spares such as ball bearings, v-belts, oil seals, springs etc.

Purpose of Holding Stocks/Inventories

The very basic purpose of inventory management is to ensure the adequate flow of inventories to the production process. There are several motives behind holding inventories. They may be speculative and non-speculative motives. But generally the seasonal factors, price and demand for the finished product determine the level of holding stocks. Samuel Elson highlights the following purposes of holding the stocks:

1. To Create a Buffer between Input and Output

Consumption of materials either may be continuous or may consist of a series of instantaneous withdrawals of batches from the stores, depending on the type of manufacture, on the process, and sometimes on the stock-control system in operation. In chemical and allied industries, where flow of materials is an integral part of the process, supply from the stores is often continuous, while in firms manufacturing engineering products and consumer goods, the assembly line is often fed by small batches of parts, designed to last for a preplanned production period. The supply of materials or components to the stores is, however, almost invariably carried out in batches, so that the stock level increases instantaneously by periodical orders for replenishment. The basic difference between the flow characteristics into and from the store compels the firm to hold inventories, which are designed to meet the needs of the production departments until new stock arrives.

2. To Ensure Against Delays In Deliveries

A batch of incoming materials is intended to last a certain period of time. When an order for fresh stock is made, supply is normally not immediately available, but sometime elapses before it arrive. This replenishment period (or 'lead-time', as it is often called) between the time of placing the order and the time of stock arrival is often subject to some variations. Since it depends very much on how heavy the production or delivery schedule is at the vendor's end, on the queue for orders that he has to meet and on the priority system operating in his organization. A manufacturing enterprise must therefore hold some reserve stocks to allow production operations to continue if delay in procurement occurs.

3. To Allow for a Possible Increase in Output if So Required

Changes in the manufacturing programme may occur because of variations in market requirements, seasonal or stochastic. While production rate cannot always be rigidly geared to demand for the product in the market (and this incidentally, is why stocks of finished products must also be held) this rate may have to be stepped up or reduced from time to time and if increased production should be allowed to proceed without interferences reserve stocks of materials must be held.

4. To Take Advantage of Quantity Discounts

Materials and components may be cheaper when purchased in larger quantities owing to larger discounts and lower transportation costs. Furthermore paper work and inspection of incoming goods are often simplified when larger quantities are ordered. On the other hand, capital is tied up in dormant goods more store space and more handling and maintenance of the goods in the store are required and greater losses due to deterioration and obsolescence are normally expected.

5. To Ensure Against Scarcity of Materials In The Market

Sometimes there are wild fluctuations in the output of certain materials and in the demand for them, so that materials may become scarce and difficult to get. A reserve stock held by the firm will ensure that production operations are not affected by sporadic scarcities in the market. During periods of rapid economic expansion or during periods of emergency, the availability or scarcity of materials would very often become a prime mover in stock control policy.

6. To Utilize the Advantage of Price Fluctuations

Price fluctuations of materials may have a marked effect on the procurement policy of a company. If these fluctuations are to be used to some advantage, materials have to be purchased in adequate quantities when prices are low. Industries depending on raw materials, especially basic materials, have to pay a great deal of attention to market prices and some firms feel that they are so dependent on price fluctuations that major policy decisions and the firm's resources become fully geared to the activities of the purchasing department.

In addition to the above Lockyer shows the following purposes of holding stocks:

7. To Meet Expected Customer Demand

A customer can be a person who walks in off the street to buy a new stereo. If the person who walks into the store discovers the stereo wanted is out of stock, he probably will head straight to a competitor's store to get it, and the sale will be lost. Similarly, if a step in a manufacturing process is delayed due to lack of parts from the previous operation, this will increase costs and possibly create additional delays down the line. In most instances, expected demand requirements are based on forecasts.

8. To Smooth Production Requirements

Firms often build up inventories in anticipation of seasonal increases in demand, and produce for inventory during off-season periods.

9. To Decouple Internal Operations

Unless successive operations have a buffer of in - process inventories between them, they will be so dependent on each other that a breakdown in any one operation or in the connecting supply links will cause the entire system to grind to a halt as individual operations shut down one after the other due to the absence of materials to work on. Conversely, unless parts are used as fast as they are produced, there must be allowances made for temporary storage.

10. To Take Advantage of Economic Lot Sizes

In order to minimize purchasing and inventory costs, it is often necessary to buy quantities that exceed immediate usage requirements. This necessitates storing some or the entire purchased amount for later use. Similarly, it is usually economical to produce in large quantities rather than small quantities. Again, the excess output must be stored for later use. Hence, inventory storage enables a firm to buy and produce in economic lot sizes without having to try to match purchases or production with demand requirements in the short run.

ABC Analysis (Always Better Control)

ABC Analysis underlines a very important principle "Vital few: Trivial many". It is equally based on the concept 'Thick on the best and thin on the rest'.

For effective inventory control, a decision has to be made that which items need little control and which need more careful control. The items of an inventory can be categorized as:

- Items, which are functionally critical to the operations; no matter, how little they cost
- Items those are important because their usage value is high;
- Items having average usage value;
- Items, which have, low usage value.

It focuses attention on those items where more savings can be expected. It is based on Pareto's law that a few high usage value items constitute a major part of the capital invested in inventories whereas bulk of inventory items having low usage value constitute insignificant part of the capital. The concept is based upon selective control, when there are large numbers of items to be analyzed then sampling may be done for ABC analysis.

Its importance lies in the determination of priority, which enables management to exercise control over inventories according to the priority fixed for the purpose on selective basis since it is neither possible nor worthwhile to pay equal attention to all the inventories in an organization. Thus, controlling the costs of only few items of inventory (A category items) will contribute to an effective control of a large amount of costs.

In the ABC inventory control system inventory is classified into high-value (Class A), medium value (Class B), and low-value (Class C). Obviously, this system does not have to be limited to three categories but this is the usual practice. Magee and Boodman have divided inventory into the following three categories:

Class A: The top 5 to 10 per cent of items, which accounts for the highest inventory investment.

Class B: The top 20 to 30 per cent of items, which accounts for a moderate share of the inventory investment.

Class C: The large remaining group of items, which accounts for a small fraction of total investment.

The key difference in the handling of these parts is that large reserve stocks should be established for class 'C' items so that there is never a possibility of running short. On 'A' items, the reserve quantities should be held to a minimum in order to decrease the investment in inventories. Thus, the main objective is the control of a small percentage of items, which account for a very large percentage of annual consumption, while the rest of the items can be virtually 'decontrolled'.

Steps in Conducting ABC Analysis

The following steps must be followed for conducting ABC Analysis:

- Prepare the list of the items and estimate their annual consumption (units).
- Determine unit price (or cost) of each item.
- Multiply each annual consumption by its unit price (or cost) to obtain its annual consumption in rupees (annual usage).

- Arrange items in the descending order of their annual usage starting with the highest annual usage down to the smallest usage.
- Calculate cumulative annual usages and express the same as cumulative usage percentages. Also express the number of items into cumulative item percentages.
- Plot cumulative usage percentages against cumulative item percentages and segregate the items into A, B, and C, categories.

The various stages where ABC Analysis can be applied are:

- Information of items, which require higher degree of control
- Evolving useful re-ordering strategy
- Stock records
- Priority treatment to different items
- Determination of safety stock limits
- Stores layout
- Value analysis

An average pattern of percentage of items and percentage of their annual use value may be worked out as follows:

ABC Analysis of Inventory

Class	Percentage of Items	Percentage of Annual use
A	10	80
B	20	15
C	70	05

From this figure and tabulated data, it is clear that 'A' category items which form only 10 per cent of the total number of items have the highest value among all the items, whereas 'C' category items, which constitutes 70 per cent of the total number of such items forms only 5 per cent of the total value.

Selective Control for ABC Classification

Sl. No.	Basis	'A' Items	'B' Items	'C' Items
1.	Control	Tight	Moderate	Loose
2.	Requirements	Exact	Exact	Estimated
3.	Postings	Individual	Individual	Group or
4.	Check	Close	Some	Little
5.	Expediting	Regular	Some	No
6.	Safety Stocks	Low	Medium	Large

Classification of Inventories

Value (Rs.) Per Unit	Volume Per Year	Category
High	High	A
High	Medium	A
Medium	High	A
High	Low	B
Medium	Medium	B
Low	High	B
Medium	Low	C
Low	Medium	C
Low	Low	C

Policy Difference Between ABC Items

Point of difference	Items A	Items B	Items C
1	2	3	4
Value	High	Moderate	Low
Safety stock	No or very Low	Low	High
Ordering frequency	Frequent; usually weekly	Monthly or quarterly	Half yearly

(Contd...)

1	2	3	4
Control reports	Weekly	Monthly	Quarterly
Follow-up action	Maximum	Periodical	Exceptional
Value analysis	Rigorous	Moderate	Minimum
Source of supply	Many rather maximum	Reliable but Lesser number of suppliers	Reliable but minimum possible
Forecasts	Accurate	Estimates	Rough estimates
Surplus and obsolescence	Nil or minimum possible	Quarterly control and review	Annual control and review
Purchasing	Centralized	Combined	Decentralized
Storage	Centralized	Combined	Decentralized
Lead-time	Minimum	Moderate	As required
Handling	By middle or top level management	By middle level management	By operating Staff
Attention	Constant	Periodic	Least

Precautions in Implementing ABC Analysis

Degree of Control

'A' items, account for bulk of the annual usage value and hence must attract utmost attention. Someone at the senior management level should be made responsible for regular reviewing of these items. Up-to-date and accurate records should be maintained for these items. The inventory should be kept at minimum by placing open orders (or orders covering annual requirement) and arranging supplies in staggered lots. Every attempt should be made to reduce both internal and external lead-time by closer follow-up at the home plant, better vendor-vendee relations and market research for alternate sources of supply.

'B' items should be brought under normal control made possible by good record keeping and periodic attention.

Little control is required for 'C' items. Replenishment work should be delegated to the lower level, who may be directly in charge of stores. This helps to bypass the red tape. Large inventories should be maintained to avoid stock outs. Individual postings should be replaced by group postings.

Quite a number of inexpensive 'C' items can be placed in a convenient spot in the stock-room or on the shop floor to enable shops to help themselves. This may look encouraging pilferage and wastage but the cost of wastage will be much less as compared to saving in time and effort otherwise spent by the stores personnel.

Ordering Procedure

'A' items require careful and accurate determination of order quantities and order points based on exact requirements. They should be subjected to frequent reviews to reduce unwarranted stock outs possibility of overstocking. A reasonable good analysis for order quantities and order points is required for B items but the stocks may be reviewed less frequently.

No such computations are necessary for C items. These items should be bought in bulk. Their stocks may be reviewed only when major changes occur.

Staggering of Delivery Schedule

Staggering of delivery schedules is one of the best strategies to reduce the inventory investment and ensure uninterrupted inflow of materials. Staggered deliveries tend to reduce cost of order writing but increase the cost of inspection and receiving. Annual contract with scheduled deliveries are desirable for A and B class of items. 'C' class of items however, should be purchased in bulk on single-order-basis.

Stock Records

Detailed records of goods ordered, received, issued, and goods on hand need to be maintained for A category of items. Tight control and accurate records are also required for scrap, loss and rejection of such items.

No such detailed records are necessary for C items. Normal office procedure is sufficed. Two-bin-system is most suitable for these items.

Any routine method that ensures good and accurate records is enough for B category of items.

Priority Treatment

VIP treatment may be accorded to A items in all activities such as processing of purchase orders, receiving, inspection, movement on the shop floor, etc., with an object to reduce lead-time and average inventory.

No such treatment is necessary for B items. However plant producers should take care of inward and outward flow of these items. However, "control by exception" may be exercised for critical items.

Ordinarily, no priority is assigned to C items. Personnel at the lower level should be able to take care of these items.

Safety Stock

All items of consumption are equally important from production point of view. Shortages do occur even when accurate and realistic order points have been computed. Safety stock is provided to safeguard against these shortages. Safety stock should be less for 'A' items. The possibility of stock-outs can considerably be cut down by closer forecasting, frequent reviewing and more progressing. C items, on the contrary, should have sufficient safety stock to eliminate progressing and to reduce the probability of stock outs. A moderate policy is required for B items, safety stock being neither too high nor too low.

Price Discounts

Many manufacturers offer discounts if more units are ordered. A decision, therefore, has to be made whether to strictly follow the pre-fixed order quantity or raise the same to take advantage of price discount.

Stores' Layout

ABC Analysis can be efficiently utilized for the store's layout as well. Quite a bit of time and effort can be saved which otherwise is lost in locating fast moving items near the point of issue. Most of these items will belong to A category. B items, which are less active, can be put slightly farther.

Most of the C items can be put in the less accessible areas except those, few which might have fallen in C category because of their low consumption. Such items may also be located in readily accessible areas.

Physical Stock-Taking

The process of physical stocktaking can be made more efficient by the application of usage value classification. Ordinarily, all the items are subjected to 100 per cent check with the same frequency. This is time consuming, laborious and leads to production stoppages. It is not necessary to have a uniform policy of physical stock-taking for all the items.

'A' items may be checked more often and C items, on the contrary, least often. One of the decisions could be to check A items every two months, B items every three months and C items every six months.

Value Analysis

To secure maximum benefits, it is essential to select those items for value analysis, which offer the highest scope for cost reduction. The usage value classification (ABC Analysis) is a useful step in this direction. Only A and B items are selected for detailed value analysis, and the former is given priority over the later. C items should not be value analyzed.

Self-learning Activity

Try to answer the following questions on your own:

1. What does inventory management mean?
2. What are the essentials of inventory management?
3. Write notes on: *(a)* work-in-process; *(b)* supplies?
4. Explain steps involved in ABC analysis?

Summary

- Inventory management is part of the materials management, which is a deciding factor for cost reduction measures in organizations.
- Inventory management tells the organization the quantities to be ordered and the type of material to be ordered and explains the process of cost saving.
- Inventories are classified into various categories like raw materials, supplies, production inventories, in-process inventories, materials in transit, and dealers' stock.
- Organizations keep a sizeable stock in order to avoid production loss. Continuous supply of materials must be guaranteed to the production department by the inventory department.
- The ABC analysis explains the type of investment to be made on materials and saving of money by means of avoiding locking of capital in unnecessary items.

Inventory Control and Classifications 8

Techniques of Inventory Control

Importance of Inventory Control

- It ensures balanced flow of materials, components, tools, equipment and other articles.
- Minimizes stock out, (i.e., couple finishing of stock) which causes interruption of production or break down of operation.
- It reduces possibility of excess items being locked up in storage. Large inventories mean locked up capital. There is also the danger of obsolescence, (i.e., material becoming out dated due to change in their design or arrival of better quality material).
- Inventory control minimizes investment on inventories.
- This lead to lowest storage or inventory carrying cost.
- It produces saving in purchases through evaluation of requirements on scientific basis.
- It eliminates duplication in ordering or replenishing the stocks.
- It permits better utilization of available stocks by transforming them from one department to another one requiring it.
- It provides a check against a pilferage or loss of materials through carelessness or misappropriation.

- It facilitates accounting of cost by laying down a best system for allocating material costs to products.
- It necessitates simplified procedures for paper work and record keeping which cut down delays and confusion in procuring and supplying materials.
- It also serves as a means for location and disposal of inactive or obsolete items of store.
- It applies modern management techniques such as standardization value and analysis, waste control and import substitution which cut down the material costs and simplifies their storage, handling and issue and record keeping.
- It provides a constant and reliable basis for financial statements.
- Inventory control, therefore finally results in reduced manufacturing cost and working capital, thus increasing profitability of an undertaking.

Techniques of Inventory Control

There are two types of inventory control systems, namely *(i)* Basic Systems and *(ii)* Selection Control Systems. Lee and Dobler employ the following in controlling inventories:

(a) The cyclical ordering system;

(b) The fixed order quantity system;

(c) The material requirements planning system (MRP);

(d) Economic Order Quantity (EOQ).

A. Cyclical Ordering System

This is a time-based system, which involves scheduled periodic reviews of the stock level of all inventory items. When the stock level of a given item is not sufficient to sustain the production operation until the next scheduled review, an order is placed replenishing the supply. The frequency of reviews varies from firm to firm, depending upon the importance of the materials, specific production schedules, market conditions, and so forth. Order quantities likewise vary for different materials. For administrative convenience, however, each material's order quantity is usually chosen from a small number of predetermined coverage periods.

Stock levels can be monitored by physical inspection, by a visual review of perpetual inventory cards, or by automatic computer surveillance. In operations where a small number of materials are involved, the simplest and most accurate method is a periodic physical count of the stock. Where this is not practical, as is the case with most firms of substantial size, a perpetual inventory record for each material can be maintained (manually or by computer) by posting receipts from invoices and disbursements form stores material requisitions. If this procedure is closely controlled, the inventory record for each material should at all times be in reasonable close agreement with the actual stock balance. Human errors inevitably creep into such a procedure, however, necessitating a physical stock count at least once or twice in a year.

In practice, the cyclical ordering system is well suited for materials whose purchases must be planned months in advance because of established and infrequent production schedules maintained by the suppliers. It also works well for materials which exhibit an irregular or seasonal usage and whose purchases must be planned in advance on the basis of sales estimates.

The system can, of course, be used for all materials in an inventory. However, it possesses three disadvantages. First, it compels a periodic review of all items; this in itself makes the system somewhat inefficient. Because of differences in usage rates, many items may not have to be ordered until the succeeding review. Conversely, the usage of some items during the period may have increased to the point where they should have been ordered before the current review date. Consequently, this system must be augmented with a minimum balance figure which signals the need for an early reorder in the case of a sharp usage increase.

Second, and equally important, the system demands the establishment of rather inflexible order quantities in the interest of administrative efficiency. Theoretically, there exists an optimum economic order quantity for each item, depending upon its price structure, its rate of usage, and attendant internal costs. However, because all items must fit reasonably well into a limited number of ordering cycles under this system, actual order quantities may deviate substantially from the optimum. For a given materials, the net effect frequently is at increase in the total inventory costs associated with that item.

Finally, the cyclical ordering system tends to peak the purchasing workload around the review dates. This disadvantage can be avoided to some extent by regulating the frequency of reviews. In practice, though, it is difficult indeed to smooth the load of the desired level.

Flow Control System

The 'flow control' method of managing inventories represents a special variation of the cyclical system. This special method is applicable in continuous manufacturing operations, which produce the same basic product in large quantities day after day. Most materials used in such an operation are purchased on term contracts and scheduled for daily or weekly delivery throughout the term. The production cycle is often a day or less in duration and, in effect, material flows through the plant in continuous streams.

Inventory flows consequently can be kept quite low, thus requiring a minimum investment in production inventory. In such an operation, stores personnel daily review visually the level of all material stocks and report any imbalances to the purchasing or production control department. Changes in production schedules must be relayed immediately to buyers so that delivery schedules can be revised accordingly.

B. Fixed Order Quantity System (FOQ)

A second basic type of inventory control system—the fixed order quantity system—is based on the order quantity factor rather than on the time factor. The design of this system recognizes that each item possesses its own unique order quantity, and, in practice, the system permits more effective utilization of this fact.

Operation of a fixed order quantity system warrants the following conditions:

- The predetermination of a fixed quantity to be ordered each time so that the supply of the item is replenished. This determination typically is based on a consideration of price, rate of usage, and other pertinent production and administrative factors.
- The predetermination of an order point, so that when the stock level on hand drops to the order point, the item is automatically 'flagged' for reorder purposes. The order point, is computed so that estimated usage of the item during the order lead-time period will cause the actual stock level to fall to a planned minimum stock level by the time the new order is received. Receipt of the new order then increases the stock level to a planned maximum figure.

The automatic feature of the system is achieved most commonly by maintaining a perpetual inventory record for each item carried in stock. An inventory issues until the balance of an item falls to its order point. At this time the clerk of the computer notifies the purchasing department. If the system operates correctly, purchasing replenishes the stock so that inventory levels for all items automatically remain between the planned minimum and maximum levels. The person responsible for inventories thus utilizes the management—by-exception principle in controlling them because no action is taken until action is required (i.e., until the order point is reached).

The major advantages claimed by the system are:

- each material can be procured in the most economical quantity;

- purchasing and inventory control personnel automatically devote attention to the items that need it only when required; and
- positive control can easily be exerted to maintain total inventory investment at the desired level simply by manipulating the planned maximum and minimum levels.

The system also possesses several severe limitations. It functions correctly if each of the materials exhibits reasonably stable usage and lead-time. When these factors change significantly, a new order quantity and a new order point must be determined if the system is to fulfill its objectives. Consequently, the system becomes extremely cumbersome to operate effectively when applied to materials with unstable usage patterns and lead-times. As with any system using a perpetual inventory record, errors in posting and in the issuance of stores requisitions occasionally distort book balances and may lead to undetected material shortages.

C. Material Requirements Planning (MRP) System

Widespread use of computer-based planning and control systems has greatly increased management's ability to analyze and manipulate large volumes of data to produce more timely and accurate information for decision-making purposes. In certain types of manufacturing firms, this data-handling revolution has spawned the development of a third type of production/inventory planning system. It is currently known as Material Requirements Planning, or MRP.

Re-order Level (ROL)

Receiving and issuing of inventories are the common and recurring phenomena in a manufacturing organization. When the inventories fall below a particular level, they are replenished by the fresh purchases. The prescription of re-order level (ROL) is an important technique of inventory control. It fundamentally deals with 'When to order' to replenish the inventories. Re-order level is a predetermined point, and when the existing stock of inventories reaches this point or falls below it, the purchase action is initiated to replenish them. The ROL is mentioned in the bin-card of each inventory item. What should be the quantity of replenishment order is also a matter of policy. Generally, size of the order is determined on the basis of the economic ordering quantity (EOQ), which is also an important technique of inventory control.

The re-order level is decided for each important item of inventory on the basis of following considerations:

- Lead-time
- Average periodic consumption (say, daily consumption)
- Safety stock

> Re-order level is decided as:
>
> ROL = (lead-time x average daily consumption) + Safety stock

The Re-order Level is controlled by the following techniques:

1. Two bin system

Under this system, the inventory item is divided into two parts. One part is active one from which issues are made. The other part is kept reserved and touched only when the active part is exhausted. It is also known as the 'bin reserve' system. When the reserve part is touched, a fresh order is placed to replenish the stock. The reserve part becomes active and the earlier active part, which is exhausted, is replenished with the fresh stock. The fresh order is placed for the fixed quantity. The quantity in the reserve part serves as a reordering level. It is not necessary to provide for two separate bins. Even a line can segregate the two parts. This method is applicable to low cost, high volume items, which have consistent usage. This method does not involve any record keeping.

2. Mini-Max system

Under this system, when the inventory items reaches to a predetermined minimum level, it is replenished by the fresh purchases up to the predetermined maximum level. The minimum level serves as a reordering point. The fresh order is placed for that much quantity, which shows deficiency in maximum level. Thus, the size of the order is variable rather than fixed. Like the two bin system, this method is applicable to low-cost, high-volume parts with consistent usage.

3. Impress system

Under this system, the reordering is made at regular time intervals. The maximum level of each item is predetermined. At a particular fixed period, say after one week, a fresh collective order for all the times will be placed. The size of the order will be decided on the basis of the shortages indicated by the existing stock in relation to the maximum level. Thus, the quantity of replenishment will exactly equate the quantity consumed during the period. The size of the order will vary considerably.

4. Economic Order Quantity (EOQ)

Inventory control fundamentally deals with the two basic issues. They are (i) When to order and (ii) how much to order. The problem of 'when to order' is decided by prescribing the reorder level of each of the inventory item. The other incidental issue is 'how much to order', is decided on the basis of "Economic Order Quantity (EOQ)". (*More details on EOQ are given in Chapter 9*).

Identification of Inventories and Codification

Basically the functions of inventories are two fold. They are:

1. Maintaining the required quantities of inventories, and
2. Ensuring the free flow of inventories to the production process or to the market.

For this purpose, Stephen Love identifies the following functions of inventories.

1. Market Exploitation

Often the vagaries of the market create an economic advantage for maintaining an inventory. Price fluctuations of supply may dictate premature acquisition. Anticipation of a future increase in selling price suggests a delay in disposing of stock on hand. Conversely, declining market prices are a motivation for creating a negative inventory. Such market advantages are certainly not confined to material prices. A pending increase in labour costs may make it advantageous to stock finished goods. Market exploitation is often associated with speculation, but many market conditions are sufficiently determinable to render this connotation unfounded.

2. Protection against Stock-outs

To the extent that the supply or demand process fluctuates unpredictably, there is the risk of running out of stock and suffering the associated customer strife, disruption of operations, expediting costs, etc. So-called buffer stocks provide insurance against such stock outs. The need for such stocks increases as the time between the occurrence of the random fluctuation and the compensation for it increases (by obtaining the necessary replacement stock) and also, of course, as the fluctuations increase.

3. Operations Smoothing

Demand processes are typically subject to foreseeable (but not entirely controllable) rate change. This fluctuation is usually synchronous with the season of the year or with the phenomenon of the business cycle. Although such fluctuation can be accommodated in other ways, such as changing production rates, there is usually the alternative of producing and storing in anticipation of peak demands. Just as with buffer stocks, smoothing stocks may also accommodate known fluctuations in supply.

4. Lot-size Economy

Even if it were possible to maintain supply and demand processes, which were equal and time- invariant, usually it would not be desirable to do so. This is because supply of goods at a constant rate implies a large number of deliveries with a small number of items per delivery. This would disregard the economics associated with a smaller number of deliveries and a larger number of items per delivery. If the supply process involves shipment and receipt of goods from an outside supplier, the economy basically arises from lower shipping and delivery costs. In some cases, this may consist of a supplier's offer of a quantity discount on large orders. If the supply process is internal production, economy accrues from fewer machine setups. In either case, there will likely be fewer materials handling effort and paperwork if there is fewer replenishment of stock.

5. Control System Economy

An often-overlooked purpose for carrying larger inventories is that less control effort is required. Inventory control systems are costly to design, implement, and maintain A lower-cost, "looser" mode of control, with attendant larger stocks, may be justified.

Codification

There should, be some means of identifying inventories so that proper purchasing, inspection, storing, issuing, handling and control can be done smoothly. To facilitate identification and provide a unique nomenclature to each inventory item, the techniques of codification, classification, standardization and simplification are practiced.

Codification is "a process of operating each item by a number, the digits of which indicate the group, the sub-group, the type and the dimension of the item". Rationalized codification reveals a large number of identical items stored in separate bins under different names. In fact, "this is the starting point of standardization and variety reduction programme". P.S. Rao says "apart from inventory control, the work of rationalization, variety reduction and standardization also gets greatly facilitated by a well designed and well governed material code".

Codification is necessary for all materials at all stages in manufacture as opportunities for error and confusion are too numerous; moreover, complete word descriptions are much too long and cumbersome for everyday use. For effective inventory management raw materials, stores, semi-finished materials and finished goods must all be included in any system of codification. Such identification through codification saves lot of time. Codification is also an effective means for enabling stock record section to prepare intelligent reports rapidly and correctly. These reports are, the control element in effective inventory management.

There are various types of codes, for example, sequence codes, block codes, group classification codes, decimal codes, significant digit codes, final digit codes, consonant codes, alphabetical codes, etc. Nevertheless, codes may be classified into three broad categories, depending upon the 'characters' used in the code viz.:

(a) Alphabetical code (e.g., L.K T).

(b) Numerical Code (e.g., 005-00 455) and

(c) Alpha-Numerical Code (052 ST 25455)

Coding System

The characteristics of a satisfactory coding system are:

- Any 'code-name' should indicate only one item
- Any item should bear only one code-name
- Coverage should be adequate and comprehensive
- It should be wholly numerical
- A code-name should be of constant length
- A code-name should not be excessively long
- The simpler the item, the simpler the code-name
- Classification should be by permanent features

One such numbering system is the family name - Christian name method. Each family will be given a number (the family name) and each component in that family will be given a second number (the Christian name) differentiating it from its fellows. Then, if a new component appears to be required, an examination of the drawings of the family to which it belongs is made, and suitable components selected.

Many more formal systems have been invented, fulfilling some or all of the desirable characteristics. Four systems are briefly described here:

(a) The Brisch system(UK)

(b) The Mitrofanov system(USSR)

(c) The Opitz system (W. Germany)

(d) The Vuoso system (Csechoslovakia)

The Brisch System

This requires an eight-digit primary code or mono code which effectively sets down the design characteristics of the part, followed by a secondary code, or poly code, identifying the manufacturing characteristics. Usually the first digit of the primary code is derived from the series.

- Organization and operations
- Primary materials
- Bought-out commodities
- Components
- Sub-assemblies and products
- Tools and portable equipment
- Plant and machinery
- Buildings services, utilities
- Scrap and waste
- Reserved

All other digits are 'tailor-made' to the client organization. The polycode requires reference to a 'code-book', which again will be 'tailor-made' to the user's need.

The Mitrofanov System

S.P. Mitrofanov, one of the earliest known workers in-group technologies, who first conceived the idea of the composite component, created this system. It is essentially a production-orientated code of seven digits.

First digit	(0-9)	Section	
Second digit	(0-9)	Class	Parts characterized by common function and structural shape
Third digit	(0-9)	Sub-class	Parts characterized by common shapes and similar processing methods
Fourth digit	(0-9)	Group	Characterized by similar shapes and number of manufacturing operations
Fifth digit	(0-9)	Type	Operation type
Sixth, and seventh	(0-9)	Size	

(*No reference has been found to the use of this code outside the USSR*)

The Opitz System

Opitz, working at Achen University, investigated the requirements of machine tools needed to produce the parts used by industry in West Germany. In doing so he found a need to devise a coding system, which is the opitz system. It is applicable only to machine parts, and uses five digits to define shape, followed by four 'Optional extra' digits specifying size, material, original shape of raw materials and accuracy. The complete code is contained on eight quarto sheets, and it is stated that it can be used with reasonable confidence after several hours' tuition. The code is so comprehensive that it is unlikely that any single organization will ever use more than a small part of the available identifiers, and this may result in an apparent loss of cohesiveness.

The Vuoso System

This was developed in the Vuoso Research Institute for Machine Tools and Metal Cutting in Csechoslovakia in 1959. It is a simple, four-digit code, all details of which are contained on a single sheet of paper.

Inevitably it lacks the detail of the Brisch or Opitz systems, but its simplicity is such that it should be carefully considered. Before a component is placed into a family, it is necessary to refer to the appropriate drawing-an unnecessary act with Brisch system.

Whatever the classification system used, it is important that it should be clearly defined, and that the numbers should have only one meaning, that is, they should be unique. In a small company or one where the total number of items to be classified is small, it is probably unwise to attempt too great an elaboration with the code number; however, the benefits of changing from a random coding to a logical coding are so great that the apparent difficulties in changing code numbers, even with all the attendant upheaval in renumbering in stores, in the design department, in the cost office, should be accepted and a logical system installed

Standardization

A standard is defined as a model or general agreement of a rule established by authority, consensus or custom, created and used by various levels of interest. Standardization is required not only for ensuring procurement of the right quality of incoming material but also for cost reduction. It will be remembered that considerable publicity was given to the large scale cost reduction in materials cost through standardization by the U.S. defense services under the guidance of the then Defense Secretary Robert S McNamara.

Importance of Standardization

1. Standardization enables the store keeper to achieve over all economy and ensures inter-changeability of parts.

2. Since more than one manufacturer can supply standard items it will imply better availability, better price and better delivery.
3. It creates healthy competition and ensures better quality.
4. There is need for less stock an hence less chances of obsolescence.
5. It means less inspection efforts. In fact, there is no need of inspecting routine items bearing ISI mark.
6. It is also possible to enter into rate/running contract with standard items.
7. At the suppliers end manufacturing into economic lot sizes is not a problem for standard items.

The remarks of the committee on public undertakings in regard to variety reduction are worth noticing:

The process of standardization logically leads to simplification or variety reduction. This implies reducing unnecessary varieties and standardizing to the most economical sizes, grades, shapes, colours, types of parts, and so on. In large organizations handling 50,000 items there are several items under stock having very little varieties in quality dimension or functional effectiveness, Nevertheless these continue to be in stock for historical reasons. Practical experience indicates that often this plethora of variety is not even perceptible.

These items can be analyzed by their frequency of usage or movement analysis over the last few years. Frequency or movement analysis would bring out items, which are seldom used or not used at all. On the basis of this analysis a company could set standards to replace these items. The setting up of a standard depends on the effect the dimension variation has on the performance of the product.

Self-learning Activity

Try to answer the following questions on your own:

1. Discuss about cyclical ordering system of inventory control?

2. What is codification?
3. Describe the importance of standardization?

Summary

- Inventory control ensures balanced flow of materials, components, tools and equipments to the needed sections.
- It avoids stock out, which causes interruption in production or breakdown of operation.
- Inventory control minimizes investment on inventories and leads to lowest storage or inventory carrying cost.
- There are various techniques of inventory control namely, the cyclical ordering system, fixed order quantity system, materials requirement planning, and economic order quantity.
- Organizations keep quite large number of materials and they have to be identified. Such identification process is called as coding. There are four major coding systems available for the materials manager.
- Organizations have to give importance to standardization also. Standardization enables the store keeper to achieve overall economy. It creates healthy competition among the suppliers and ensures better quality of materials.

Order Quantity 9

Economic Order Quantity

Inventory control fundamentally deals with the two basic issues. They are: *(i)* When to order; and *(ii)* how much to order. The problem of 'when to order' is decided by prescribing the reorder level of each of the inventory item. The other incidental issue is 'how much to order', is decided on the basis of 'Economic Order Quantity (EOQ)'.

If a concern buys in large-size quantities, cost of carrying the inventory shall be high because of the high investment involved. On the other hand, if purchases are made in small quantities, frequent orders with corresponding high ordering costs will result in. Therefore, the quantity to order at a given time must be determined by balancing two factors—the acquisition cost and the cost of processing the inventory. Purchases in large quantities may decrease the unit cost of acquisition, but this saving may be more than off-set by the cost of carrying inventories in godowns for a longer period of time. Thus, the ideal quantity of a material to be purchased at a time is determined by balancing the two costs—he Ordering cost and the Carrying cost.

Ordering cost is more or less fixed and it is ascertained on per order basis. If the annual requirements are met by placing more orders of small quantity instead of single large order, the number of orders placed during the year will increase resulting into higher total ordering cost.

The other side of the scene is the inventory carrying cost, when inventories are stored, it involves following types of costs:

1. Interest cost due to locking up of funds
2. Cost of storage space
3. Cost of insurance and taxes

As all these costs are directly related with the certain percentage of value of materials stored; e.g. say carrying cost is 15 per cent, i.e. 15 per cent of the value of materials stored. The ordering cost and the carrying cost is mutually exclusive. If the annual requirements are met by placing a single large order, the ordering cost will be less due to single order. But as the single order will be for a huge quantity (i.e., for the entire annual requirements), the average stockholding would be very high resulting into greater carrying cost. The relationship of ordering cost and carrying cost is as under:

Relationship between Ordering cost and Carrying cost

No.	Number and size of order	Ordering cost	Carrying cost
A	Few orders, each order of large size	Low	High
B	More orders, each order of small size	High	Low

The purpose of EOQ model is, to arrive at the 'least cost, for procuring and carrying costs. EOQ is that order quantity which will minimize the total variable costs of managing inventory. It uses the following terminology.

Q = Order quantity

Q = Economic order quantity (EOQ)

D = Total Demand (usage per period)

R = Re-order cost (cost to place one purchase order or make one Production set-up)

C = Carrying cost (cost to hold one unit in inventory for the period)

T = Total Inventory Cost per period.

The elementary EOQ Model assumes that demand\usage occurs at a constant rate throughout the period, that inventory replenishment occurs instantaneously (with no waiting for delivery) and that no inventory items are ever out of stock.

Purchases of size Q are made each time the balance falls to zero, with usage continuing at a uniform linear rate. The average inventory on hand will therefore be Q + 0\2, and the number of orders per period will be D\Q. Therefore, the total cost of placing orders will be equal to the number of orders placed multiplied by the cost per order (RD\Q). The total carrying cost will be the average number of units in inventory multiplied by the carrying cost per unit (QC\2).

The technique of economic ordering quantity (EOQ) strikes a balance between the ordering cost and the carrying cost. It devices such a quantity of each order at which the total ordering cost and carrying cost would be minimum. As both these costs are mutually exclusive the total of both costs will be minimum at a point where ordering cost equates carrying cost. This situation is explained by the graph as under:

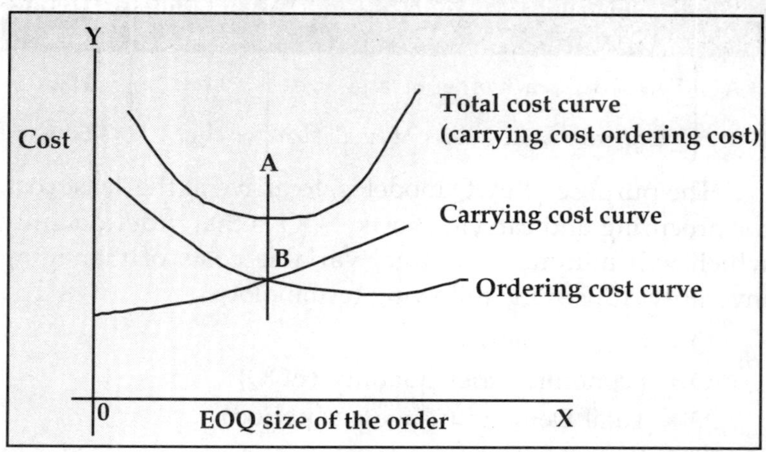

It can be seen from the above figure that 'B' indicates the size of order where:

1. The total ordering cost and carrying cost (i.e., AB) is at minimum. Any deviation from point B on left hand side

will increase ordering cost and reduce carrying cost resulting into greater cost. If the deviation is made on right hand side form point B, it will result into increase in carrying cost and reduction in ordering cost with high total cost.

2. At point, B, the ordering cost and carrying cost equates each other. Thus, B is the economic order quantity (EOQ) where the total ordering cost and carrying cost set tends to be minimum.

Inventory Pricing

The importance of inventory pricing needs to be emphasized because it contributes a significant part of the cost of production and working capital of a concern. The choice of inventory pricing method is an important decision of the management as it affects the rate and amount of cash flow into and out of the business through its effects of purchase and sales decisions. Moreover, the net profit or net loss for any period is only as accurate as the inventory values used in arriving at the profit/loss. Management uses the income and assets information, which has been influenced by the inventory pricing methods, to decide what quantity of goods to buy, when to buy them, how much to pay for them and at what price to sell them. To the extent that the inventory pricing method is unrealistic., it can lead the management to unwise decisions in these matters.

Factors Affecting the Selection of Pricing Method

No one pricing method is best suited under all conditions. Conditions including type and nature of inventory, not personal preferences, should be the base for choosing the pricing method. Neuner and Frumer have suggested the following factors to be considered in selecting a materials pricing method.

- Methods most commonly used by the industry in which engaged; this produces a sounder competition and more comparable figures.

- Frequency of price fluctuation and frequency of materials purchase.
- Relative value of materials cost to total of products manufactured.
- Frequency of raw materials purchased.
- Quantities of materials to be purchased at any one time.
- The effect of different pricing methods on income-tax.
- Trend of prices and income taxes over a long period of time.
- The possibility of using different methods for various class of inventory.

Some other factors such as nature and type of industry, length of inventory turnover period, need for reflection of current prices in cost figures, uniformity in accounting system and requirements of the relevant acts and rules.

Methods of Pricing

According to Lee and Dobler there are three basic methods by which a buyer can seek to arrive at the right price; published price lists, competitive bidding, and negotiation.

1. Published Price Lists

Published price lists in the form of daily quotations exist for standard commodities traded on the various commodity exchanges throughout the world. Price lists also exist for most standard items. Usually price lists show different prices for varying quantities. Quite often a seller who has a particular commodity in inventory will sell at a price lower than the price quoted for the commodity on the exchange. The prices shown on a seller's price list are asking prices. They may or may not be the actual selling prices.

2. Competitive Bidding

Competitive bidding is a widely discussed form of purchasing. When competitive bidding is used by private industry, requests for bids are usually sent to three to eight vendors, depending on the size of the purchase. Requests for bids ask vendors to quote the price at which they will perform in accordance with the terms and conditions of the order or contract, should they be the successful bidder. Governmental purchasers generally are not able to restrict the number of bidders to only eight. Rather, all vendors desiring to bid are permitted to do so. Under competitive bidding, industrial buyers generally, but not always, give the order to the lowest bidder. By law, government buyers are routinely required to give the order to the lowest bidder provided the lowest bidder is deemed qualified to perform the contract.

The proper use of competitive bidding, as the best method of pricing available to a buyer, is dictated by five criteria. The criteria are:

1. The value of the specific purchase is large enough to justify the expense, to both buyer and seller, which accompanies this method of purchase.
2. The specifications of the item or service to be purchased are explicitly clear to both buyer and seller. In addition, the seller knows from actual previous experience, or can estimate accurately from similar past experience, the cost of producing the item or rendering the service.
3. The market consists of an adequate number of sellers.
4. The sellers comprising the market actively want the contract and are therefore willing to price competitively to get it. Huge backlogs of work in some sellers' plants may prevent competition. Under such circumstances, additional orders would entail overtime operation and its attendant problems of scheduling difficulties and premium wage payment. Under such circumstance, if bids are made at all they are at prices that include all manner of contingencies.
5. The time available is sufficient for using this method of purchasing. Vendors competing for large contracts must

be allowed time to obtain and evaluate bids from their subcontractors before they can calculate their best price. Bidders must also have time to perform the necessary price analysis required within their own organization, and assure themselves of reliable sources of materials. The time required for preparing, mailing, opening, and evaluating bids is usually considerably longer than those unfamiliar with this system of pricing would expect.

On occasion, the government and a number of large, technically oriented firms use a modified type of competitive bidding called 'two-step bidding'. This method of pricing is used in situations where inadequate specifications preclude the initial use of regular competitive bidding. In the first step, bids are requested only for technical proposals, without any prices. Bidders are requested to set forth in their proposals technical details describing how they would produce the required materials, products, or services. After these bids are evaluated, and it is determined which proposals are technically satisfactory, the second step follows. In the second step, requests for bid are sent only to those sellers who in the first step submitted acceptable technical proposals. These sellers now complete for the business on a price basis, as they would in any routine, competitive-bidding situation.

3. Negotiation

Negotiation should be used in all situations where any one of the five mandatory criteria for competitive bidding does not prevail. When the time is too short, the value of the order is too low, the number of bidders is inadequate, their willingness to compete is lacking, or the specifications are vague, the buyer has no choice but to negotiate. By use of individual skills coupled with research findings, the buyer must attempt to answer properly the questions that lead to an intelligent source selection decision-the important questions that the competitive-bidding technique answers automatically.

Types of Inventory Pricing

Following are the types of pricing are adopted in the modern materials management.

1. First-in-first-out (FIFO) method

The principle is that issues are priced in the order of the purchase lots. The price of the earliest consignment is taken first and when that consignment is exhausted, the price of the next consignment is adopted, and so on.

First-in-first-out is the method that has been and still is more widely used that all other in the valuation of inventories. Under this method the cost of any article in the inventory is assumed to be the latest cost of the corresponding quantity purchased of produced. It is based on the assumption that the oldest material of finished goods are used or sold before using or selling any later purchases or productions, an assumption most applicable to concerns whose merchandise is subject to deterioration. This is predicated on the theory that inventory costs move towards expiration in the chronological order in which they are incurred.

The first-in-first-out method of valuing inventory clearly distorts income and fails to picture the correct cost of goods produced and sold are characterized by one or more of the following conditions:

- The inventory turnover consumes relatively long period of time because of either the length of processing or conditions of merchandising, thus necessitating the maintenance at all time of substantial inventory.
- The average investment in inventory is relatively large compared with other assets.
- The inventory consists a few basic and imperishable commodities, which are subject to wide price fluctuations.
- The cost of raw materials constitutes a substantial part of the cost of the finished product, and increase in the prices of raw materials is promptly reflected in the price of the product.

2. Base Stock Method

This is not an independent method of pricing inventory. The method is based on the principle that only a portion of the stores/materials moves and a core is always maintained in stock. This core or base stock represents the minimum balance of the materials and is computed on an estimated basis for each item. The base stock is valued usually at the lowest purchase price and the moving portion of the store over and above the base stock is priced under any of the methods.

The inventory may also be valued as per the base stock of normal stock method. This method is predicted on the theory that the only real costs are replacement cost and that a fixed, or a relatively fixed permanent quantity of inventory analogous to a reservoir, without which operations, would not be continued must be maintained at all times. This essential supply or base stock, is valued at a fixed price, usually so low that actual prices will never fall below it. "This part of the inventory is treated as though it was never sold, despite the fact that it is mixed with incoming inventory and physically more or less, does not get processed and is used with the inventory purchased during a given year, or during other accounting periods, in excess of this base stock is generally valued on the basis of cost or market whichever is lower, by the first-in-out method, or by averaging".

3. Average Price Method

The average price method differs from the other methods in that it adopts, as its basis, average cost and also when the transactions are numerous and there is a heavy fluctuation in the purchase price. Under this method, sharp price fluctuations are smoothened and movement of the issue rice, whether upward or downward, is gradual.

The following methods of averaging issue price are in use:

- Simple average method;

- Periodic simple average method;
- Moving simple average method;
- Weighted average method;
- Periodic weighted average method; and
- Moving weighted average method

The average cost is a 'moving average' and is figured from additions to and subtractions from stock on hand each month over, roughly, a three-year period. At times, inventory valuations on the balance sheet bear little relation to the immediate market prices. In order to use average cost it is quite necessary for a concern to have a complete cost system with perpetual inventory records kept in both rupee and quantities. The weighted average for an item is computed by adding the purchases to the beginning inventory and dividing the total amount by the total quantity. This weighted average cost is used in pricing, the closing inventory. This method eliminates much of the detailed pricing, spreads the effect of price fluctuations, and its is more satisfactory from the managerial point of view where costs on an average are of greater importance than are costs of a particulars lot.

4. Retail Method

This method values the inventory at average cost of market price whichever is lower. It is considered to be the most scientific and satisfactory method of valuing inventories for retail enterprises, although in recent years many of the large departmental stores have superimposed last-in-first-out on the retail method.

The retail inventory method of valuation eliminates the laborious processed of inventorying and costing thousands of items to obtain an inventory figure for balance sheet purposes. Balance sheets may be prepared monthly or as often as desired by using the book inventories obtained from the merchandise record or stock ledger. This inventory verification may be done for the store as a whole at one time or by departments or sub-divisions of department throughout the year.

5. Standard Price Method

In this method, the price of issue is pre-determined for stated period taking into account all the factors affecting price such as anticipated market trends, transportation charges, and normal quantity of purchase. Standard pries are determined for each material and materials requisitions are priced at standards irrespective of the actual purchase price. Even where standards have not been fixed or cannot be fixed, it may be possible to adopt estimated prices to serve as standards on a short-term basis. Where prices of materials fluctuate heavily, it is not practicable to fix standard prices on long-term basis under such cases they are computed for short periods only and modified frequently, as necessary.

The standard cost refers as predetermined cost computed on the specification of the product and predetermined manufacturing methods, which include specific amounts of raw materials and direct labour. It is more a theory of what cost should be than what cost really is. A standard raw material is obtained from an itemized schedule of the various kinds, grades and size of materials used. The standard labour is obtained from an itemized schedule of operations necessary for the manufacture of the product, computed at current labour rates. The difference between standard cost and actual costs is usually reflected in over-absorbed and under-absorbed accounts which are used in making actual adjustment at the time of the physical inventory.

6. Last-in-first-out (LIFO) Method

This method of pricing of inventory is done in the reverse order of purchase, i.e., by adopting the price of the latest available consignment. As the method applies the current cost of materials stores to the cost of units except when the purchases were made long ago, it is also sometimes known as the Replacement Cost Method.

'This method of inventory valuation, unlike the base stock method of pricing inventory, disregards the necessity of any given volume of inventory. It assumes that real cost of goods are those of replacement, as nearly as possible at the time of sale and, therefore, sales are cost on the basis of inventory latest acquired, or last-in, while first-in inventory is treated as unsold or, in effect, a tool for future operations, and is, thus, reported on the balance sheet. Since this method of interpreting cost does not necessarily require any fixed amount of stock, the volume of purchases and sales will affect first-in inventory at the end of any given year.

7. Market Price Method

Under this method, the market price is adopted as the basis for pricing the issues. The term market price is liable to various interpretations. It may mean the last purchase price, expected market price if purchased now, purchase or quotation price on the data of issue, net realizable value, or the replacement price of purchase made at a later date.

The market price method is useful for pricing of issues of obsolete stores and items that have been lying in stock for long periods in which case the net realizable price should be adopted as the issue price. Another important feature of the method is that if issues are priced at current market rates, price reduction, if any, on account of advance purchases in bulk is not reflected in the cost of sales.

8. Net-in First-out (NEFO) Method

Under this method, the issue price is taken as the price of the next consignment of materials that is still to arrive and is yet to be brought on charge. The purpose is to adopt a rate of issue as near as possible to the current market rate. In this respect, it is similar to the market price method but it is more simple to operate since the price of the next consignment due is readily available in the purchase order is changed at the time of actual payment after the receipt of the consignment due to any escalation clause or otherwise.

Material Requirements Planning (MRP) System

Widespread use of computer-based planning and control systems has greatly increased management's ability to analyze and manipulate large volumes of data to produce more timely and accurate information for decision-making purposes. In certain types of manufacturing firms, this data-handling revolution has spawned the development of a third type of production/inventory planning system. It is currently known as Material Requirements Planning, or MRP.

The MRP concept provides a very basic and different way of looking at the management of production inventories in an intermittent manufacturing operation. Fundamentally, MRP challenges the traditional concept that any significant level of production inventory need be carried prior to the time materials are actually required by the production schedule has been established, and product bills of material have been finalized, it is possible to calculate precisely these production materials needs for a given period of operation. The bill of material for a given finished product can be 'exploded' and extended for the number of units to be produced to obtain that product's exact requirements for each component material or part. Since a given part typically is used in more than one finished product, requirements for that part in all products can be summed up to obtain the total requirements for the part during the operating period in question. Without a computer, this 'explosion and aggregation' process is virtually impossible to do quickly and accurately in a firm producing many different products. With a properly programmed computer to process the huge volume of data, however, the task can be accomplished with relative ease.

In practice, the MRP approach calculates production material requirements weekly (based on production schedules that are updated weekly) several operating periods in advance of the actual need. It then generates requisitions for each material to be delivered in the required quantity several days prior to the staff of the manufacturing operation. In essence, the 'pure' MRP approach attempts to eliminate (minimize) most inventory requirements and gear purchasing and production activities to the timing and quantity usage demands of the final product assembly schedule.

Consider for a moment, about the operation of a cyclical ordering system. When a given item is reviewed, how does this system determine whether an order should be placed and, if it should, what quantity should be ordered? Several methods can be used, but a commonly used method is identical to the 'explosion and aggregation' method used in the MRP approach. The only difference lies in the timing of the order relative to the time that particular lot of material is required by production. The cyclical system calls for order delivery before the material is actually needed and maintains an inventory safety stock. Ideally, an MRP system times material delivery to coincide with production requirements and maintains no safety stock.

Clearly, this major element in the MRP concept has evolved from experience with the cyclical ordering system. And more refined use of the computer has produced accurate and timely data that permit MRP to eliminate, or minimize, the need for safety stock inventory. A cardinal difference between the two systems, however, is the driving force, which actuates the material acquiring cycle. In the case of the cyclical ordering system, it is the inventory control system itself that is designed to initiate the request for material. In an MRP operation the master production schedule (as updated each week) is the force that directly initiates and drives subsequent activities of the purchasing and manufacturing functions. It is this fundamental difference, which sets the MRP system apart from all other inventory control systems.

As implied earlier, the techniques of an MRP system are designed for use in certain specialized operating situations. The system can be used most advantageously under the following conditions:

- When usage (demand) of the material is discontinuous or highly unstable during a firm's normal operating cycle, an intermittent manufacturing or job-shop operation, as opposed to a continuous processing or mass production operation, typifies this situation.
- When demand for the materials is directly dependent on the production of other specific inventory items or finished products, MRP can be thought of as primarily a component fabrication planning system in which the demand for all parts (materials) is dependent on the demand.
- When the purchasing department and its suppliers, as well as the firm's own manufacturing, units, possess the flexibility to handle order placements or delivery releases on a weekly basis. Moreover, they must be able to respond effectively to sizable weekly changes in material demand requirements, without serious interference from such potential problem as unbalanced internal work loads of significant variation in supplier lead time requirements.

Advantages of MRP

Use of an MRP system has some very fundamental and far-reaching implication for performance of the purchasing and related materials management activities. MRP, in its purest form, is a requirements oriented system whose objective is to maintain virtually no inventory and to deliver materials to meet the timing requirements of the production schedule. Its major advantage, then, is that it tends to minimize inventory investment and carrying costs. In accomplishing this objective, however, it 'gives up' some of the operating advantages provided by inventory buffer stocks. Absence of such buffer stocks mandates that the various operating units, including purchasing, must gear their daily activities more closely to the fluctuating demands of the master production schedule. In short, the system itself focuses no only one element of the total materials cost equation; it does not consider variable acquisition costs or the variability of the cost of purchased materials.

In the case of purchased items, both materials and acquisition costs may well be expected to increase under MRP operation. Depending on the item, material and transportation costs frequently are influenced by order quantity, size of shipment, and the degree of flexibility of the delivery requirements imposed on suppliers. In the purchasing department itself, once MRP control is implemented, daily activities become tied more closely to fluctuating short-term production requirements. Clerical costs associated with the increased need for external transportation control, receiving, inspection, and accounting paperwork, as well as supplier expediting, obviously go up.

Consequently, if a manager wants to hold down material and acquisition costs, MRP is best suited for the control of purchased materials that exhibit the following characteristics:

- Materials that can be purchased on long-term contracts or blanket orders and be released for frequent shipment in relatively small quantities.
- Raw materials or "standard" items for which lead-time requirements are relatively short and seldom very appreciably.
- Materials that can be purchased repetitively without requiring much creative purchasing analysis, or for which value analysis, purchasing research, and vendor studies have previously been completed.

Proponents claim that to realize major benefits from an MRP system, nearly all production inventory items must be controlled by the system. For items made in the firm's own manufacturing facilities this view is valid. Determination of leading priorities and availability of capacity in the various production centers, for purposes of subsequent production scheduling, is obviously difficult if all demands on the centers are not channeled through the same control system. In the case of purchased items, however, the logic of the argument is less compelling. It appears to that it is possible to use a combination of systems, controlling some items with MRP and others with a conventional quantity - based or time-based system. If tight control and low inventory levels are required for selected high value items having one or more of the characteristics noted above, it appears that MRP control can be utilized in essentially the same way as a cyclical ordering system can be used. MRP application, of course, should be contingent on favorable results of a total cost study.

Self-learning Activity

Try to answer the following questions on your own:

1. Discuss about EOQ?
2. What are the factors affecting the selection of pricing method?
3. Write short notes on: Net-in First-out (NEFO) method?

Summary

- The quantity of materials to be purchased by an organization is decided by past consumption data and by practical experience.
- But the tool, EOQ gives the right type of quantity to be ordered by manager. This technique explains the stage at which materials could be bought at a least cost to keep the procuring and carrying cost evenly.
- There are various types of pricing techniques followed by organizations. The popular types of inventory pricing are FIFO method, average method, standard price method, LIFO method, and NEFO method.
- The MRP technique assesses the requirements of materials for different departments. Certain techniques like bill of material technique and past consumption data analysis are applied under MRP system.

Transportation

Importance of Transportation

Transport has lot of importance in materials management. This function cannot function without the importance of transport. Materials, components and finished products are moved many times during the course of production. Although transportation adds time and place utility, its value is not immediately known because it does not change the physical parameters of a product. But it is costly and considerable attention is given to the economics of transport management.

Traffic in a narrow sense is the physical movement of goods. The term physical distribution includes traffic plus inventory control, warehousing, materials handling, packaging, and related activities. Three aspects of traffic or transportation are:

(a) Mode

(b) Routings

(c) Vehicles scheduling

Routing and traffic management is a specialized field requiring in-depth knowledge of department of transport regulations and freight rates

Transport has the following importance to materials management:

- Through efficient transport, raw materials and goods can be transported from one part of the country to other part;

- The demand-supply position of goods can be managed by transport;
- The cost relating to storage could be avoided by efficient transport;
- Through transport, the area of a market can be extended to regions, and even to countries;
- Transport provides employment opportunity to a section of the population;
- Industrialization has close relation to transport industry. Factories engaged in transport vehicles provide export earnings, revenue to the government, and employment opportunity to people;
- Transport as a business gives good revenue to the government by way of taxes (road taxes);
- They provide 'place utility' and 'time utility'. Place utility denotes the fuller utilization of the place (market, market yard, etc). Time utility denotes the utilization of the time (of the farmers, merchants, etc) by all the people involved in the transport;
- For perishable raw materials like vegetables, fruits, and milk, an efficient transport system alone can market the products;
- Transport enlarges the market by means of connecting several points of the markets in a country and the scope of markets is widened;
- Transport helps the people to enjoy variety of goods including agricultural goods;
- Mobility of factors of production is ensured by transport. Migration of labor reduces the unemployment problem;
- Transport systems develop new markets and new urban centers are created;
- Transport system helps to create industrialization. The localization of industries is possible out of transport systems.

Types of Transport

For materials management, the following types of transport are available:

Road transport: Road transport is one of the convenient methods of transport available in a country. Through transport every nook and corner of the country can be connected to the market. Road transport has the following advantages:

(a) It is the most convenient transport for the farmers;

(b) A road transport can be used by cart, and modern vehicles;

(c) Road transport can be operated during all seasons in a year (rain, sun, etc.);

(d) Even big and small markets within a country can be connected by road transport;

(e) Time is saved in a road transport to load and unload commodities;

(f) Road transport is convenient for all types of activities.

Limitations of Road Transport

(a) Heavy infrastructure is needed to have good roads. So, road construction is costly.

(b) Road transport is costly compared to other types of transport.

(c) Large quantities cannot be moved through road transport.

(d) Maintenance of road should be taken every year.

(e) Due to increase in fuel price and vehicle price, the cost of road transport increases every year.

(f) The tax policies of regional governments and restrictions of movements by governments affect the working of road transport.

Water transport: Water transport is the cheapest transport compared to other methods of transport. Water transport can be divided into two types, *viz.* inland water transport and sea transport (shipping). Inland water transport is arranged by means of leveling the rivers and checking the flow of water. Water transport has the following advantages:

(*a*) Water transport is the cheapest of all transports;

(*b*) Through water transport huge quantities of goods can be transported;

(*c*) Major cities of a country with port facilities can be provided the goods in time and shortages could be avoided.

Limitations of Water Transport

(*a*) During rainy season, there will be disturbance for this transport.

(*b*) Loading and unloading will take lot of time.

(*c*) A country should have modern ports and river beds for this transport.

(*d*) Regulations of countries disturb the movement of goods.

Railways: Apart from the passenger railways, goods railways play a major role in the movement of goods in a country. For an efficient transportation through railways, heavy investment is needed apart from maintenance. Railways transport has the following advantages:

(*a*) It is one of the fastest transport next to air transport;

(*b*) Huge quantities of commodities can be transported;

(*c*) It gives good income to the railway and government;

(*d*) It creates good employment opportunity to laborers and other sections.

Limitations of Railway Transport

(*a*) Heavy investment is needed to construct new railways.

(*b*) Maintenance is the major problems of railways. Poor maintenance will lead to inefficiency and accidents.

(*c*) Lot of wastages are made during loading and unloading.

(*d*) Perishable goods cannot be transported.

Air transport: This is modern transport system, which can be operated in any country. Though air transport is meant for passenger traffic, it is broadly used for the transport of goods including agricultural commodities. Air transport has the following advantages:

(a) It is the fastest of all the transports;

(b) It can reach any country or any part of a country;

(c) Perishable goods like flowers, fruits, etc can be transported through air;

(d) It is a good mode of transport to earn foreign exchange.

Limitations of Air Transport

(a) It is the costliest method of transport.

(b) Heavy risk is involved in this system.

(c) Limited quantities alone can be transported.

(d) Heavy investment is needed to purchase the planes.

(e) It is suited to places where air station is available.

Transport Cost

Transport cost is an important variable cost that forms part of marketing. In certain goods, half of the cost would be included for marketing. To get benefits to the farmers, the cost of transport should be kept low. Factors deciding the cost of transport are as follows:

(a) *Distance:* Depending on the distance as long and short, the transport cost will be high and low.

(b) *Quantity of the Product* If the quantity of product transported is high, the transport cost will also be high.

(c) *Mode of Transport:* Depending on the type of transport, the cost varies. Water transport is the cheapest one and the air transport is the costliest one.

(d) *Nature of the Commodity.* Perishable commodities, bulky and inflammable commodities involve high transport cost.

(e) The Cost of Transport will be less if goods are arranged up and down.

(*f*) *Risk:* If heavy risk is involved (accidents, theft, etc) the cost of transport will be high.

(*g*) *Special Type of Facility:* If facilities like cold storage are needed, then the cost of transport will be high.

Self-learning Activity

Try to answer the following questions on your own:

1. Write notes on: Air Transport?
2. What is the importance of transportation?
3. Describe the factors deciding cost of transportation?

Summary

- Transport occupies a very important place in materials management.
- Speedy transport avoids loss of time and saving in costs.
- There are various types of transport systems like the road transport, water transport, air transport, and railway transport available to the materials management.
- The cheapest transport system is water transport system. But the fastest transport system is the air transport system.
- The types of transport system to be selected depend on the time factor and the urgency for the needs of the materials.

Materials Management Practices in Cooperatives

Cooperatives practice materials management concepts in their daily routine business. They are not exceptional cases. In this chapter materials management practices in cooperatives is discussed.

Procurement and Movement of Materials

Materials procurement is the important stage of materials management in cooperatives. In the case of agricultural processing cooperatives the basic raw materials are supplied by the members and the cooperative will have some control over quantity and quality. In the case of goods manufactured by a consumers' cooperative, raw materials will have to be procured from outside sources, and much depends on wise buying, right decisions on quality and price, and deliveries so timed that, while the factory is never short of material, the storerooms do not become overcrowded nor do stocks begin to deteriorate.

Materials handling is very important part of every manufacturing activity or trading business and, surprising as this may seem, may account for anything from 30 to 90 per cent of the cost of producing an article. It is therefore essential that any movement of materials within the plant should be carefully planned so that the shortest distances are travelled with the least expenditure of labour and power, and the least risk of loss or damage.

Inspection of Materials

Materials have to be inspected for quantity and quality. The work of quality control will be done by all types of cooperatives where materials are handled. Inspection at different points of the processing operation will also be necessary for an industrial product of any complexity, in order to ensure no faults are developing; and the end of product will have to be inspected before it is accepted or rejected for dispatch to customers. In addition, there will probably have to be periodic inspections of packing and containers. All this is costly, but unless it is done the cooperative risks putting faulty goods into its members' hands or on the outside market and having them returned, with a resulting loss of money and goodwill.

Stores Management

Cooperatives of all types should have store to keep materials safe. We may have an example of agricultural cooperatives using stores. There are reasons to store agricultural produces: They are:

- Most crops are harvested seasonally and consumed continually.
- Crops have to be accumulated from individual member's deliveries, until there is enough to warrant transport to a further customer.
- Crops are produced sporadically but processed on a continuous basis.
- Crops command low prices at harvest time. The cost of storage is less than the difference that can be obtained by selling them later.
- Crops for export must be accumulated until they make up a ship or aeroplane load for international transport.
- A primary co-operative society is not necessarily the most economical base for crops to be stored.
- Some crops, at some stages, may be more economically stored on the farm or by subsequent customers and processors.

- Unless crops can more economically and effectively be stored by a society, the society should allow its members or its customers to perform this function instead.

Ask trainees to write down as many different costs and risks as they can think of which make up the total cost of storage. Allow them up to fifteen minutes for this. Ask each trainee in turn for one item and continue until all suggestions have been listed on the chalkboard/OHP. Trainees may include items such as the following; ensure that the basic categories of physical facilities, risk or loss, deterioration and cost of money are all covered.

- The cost of storage buildings.
- The cost of packaging required only for storage.
- The cost of land on which buildings are built.
- The cost of equipment for moving the crops into and out of storage.
- The cost of racks or any other storage appliances.
- The cost of crop loss to unavoidable fungus, rodent attack and so on.
- The cost of decline in value because the crop is less fresh.
- The cost of insurance.
- The cost of labour for storing and putting into and withdrawing from storage.
- The cost of interest or whatever else might have been earned with the money if the crop had been sold earlier (opportunity costs).
- The risk of theft.
- The risk of fire.
- The risk of decline in value.
- The risk of other disasters such as flood and wind damage.

Dispatch of Materials

While dispatching materials, careful and alert handling is imperative. Finished articles must move smoothly out of plant. They must not accumulate in warehouses, unnecessarily taking up space; at the same time, customers' order to cost must be met promptly. The best kind of container or packing material in relation to cost must be discovered and used. It will be necessary to decide whether returnable or non-returnable containers will be more economical, what the cost of returning them will be and how many journeys they may be expected to survive before they fall to pieces. The whole question of alternative means of transport must be considered.

Maintenance of Materials

In cooperatives where business is of a seasonal nature, there will often be weeks or even months during which no products are coming in and the whole plant can be stripped down, cleaned, tested, repaired if necessary and made ready for the next season. This is not so easy where the plant runs continuously throughout the year. Some provision must, however, be made for inspection and overhaul. A faulty machine may not only cause losses through breakdown or a faulty product but also may be a source of danger to workers. Maintenance of materials and machines must be placed in the hands of someone as incharge for that activity in cooperatives. Whether or not the cooperative should employ its own skilled workers for routine maintenance work depends largely on the size of the organization. A large scale cooperative may find it worth while to keep maintenance staff. A small cooperative, which requires such persons occasionally, will do better to call in a local firm or an independent craftsman to maintain materials periodically.

Transport Function in Cooperatives

All cooperatives make use of transport, either for bringing goods into its premises, and moving them about while they are there, or for delivering them to members or markets. Well organized, economical use of transport may contribute a great deal to the success, and carelessness may give rise to delays, inefficiencies and unnecessary costs which may turn profit into loss. Even if transport between members and their cooperatives is of a simple from in the early stages, transport between the cooperatives and their markets or sources of supply is likely to be much more modern. The resources are; rail, road, air, water transports. In several countries some cooperatives have been founded when a number of farmers have grouped together to hire and fill a railway wagon. In some countries it may be possible or even necessary to use water transport—canal, river, lake or by sea. Cooperatives importing and exporting on a large scale may have a problem of finding cargo space in large ocean-going ships. However, this task is being taken over by statutory marketing boards, partly or wholly representing the producers, through which all cooperatives export their produces. Probably few cooperatives make much use of air transport, but there are certainly one or two, selling expensive and highly perishable commodities, such as flowers, fruits and vegetables, which find it profitable to have them delivered by air.

Internal Transport and Materials Handling

The movement of materials within the cooperative premises, from store to counter, the internal transport is felt much. Goods which have to be moved from lorry to store, store to counter will be moved by hand, or at most by wheelbarrow. In larger cooperatives, and particularly those handling bulk materials or products such as grains, milk or fertilizers, forma of mechanized transport are launched. Cranes and lifts powered by electricity are also used in large scale cooperatives to move goods from ground floor to stairs or so.

In deciding on the type of equipment to be installed, it will be necessary to think first of what it has to do, how it can be fitted into the existing infrastructure without using up space needed for other purposes, how much it is going to be used, purpose, cost in terms of purchasing, installation and maintenance, and eventually replace.

Transport Cooperatives

So far it has been assumed in this chapter that transport is merely one function of a cooperative having as its main purpose the marketing of produce or the distribution of supplies. However, there are cooperatives exist for the sole purpose of running transport fleet. Usually the members are the drivers of vehicles, there are also worker-owned transport cooperatives operate buses, taxicabs, vans, general service lorries. They serve cooperatives in transporting fertilizers, milk, grains, and agricultural produces on contract basis by agreement.

Transportation in Cooperatives— Cases (Source: MATCOM Training manual on Transport Management, ILO, 1981)

Failing Transport Services

Case A

The farmers of region A produce a crop that deteriorates rapidly after harvesting. They use bullock carts to carry all their produce to markets within 1 or 2 days' distance. A few years ago they increased production but found it was not worthwhile. Although they had enough time to carry the extra produce to more distant markets, the quality of the produce when it arrived was so poor that the price received did not justify the effort and expense of growing it.

Case B

The Co-operative had purchased a truck. It carried a lot of produce (and goods) quickly to and from town. The farmers, however, were not entirely satisfied. They still had to carry their produce long distances to a collection point on a main road because the unsurfaced tracks could not support the weight of the truck especially in the wet season.

Case C

The Co-operative had bought its truck about a year ago. The garage had said that they should return it every 8000 km for inspection and maintenance. They did this once or twice but stopped because it cost a lot of money and all the garage seemed to do was change the oil. Now after about a year the truck keeps breaking down. Last week the truck broke down on the way to market and, as no alternative transport could be found, the whole load of produce it was carrying went rotten and became unsalable.

Case D

One of the farmers in village D bought a new lorry. He intended to use it to convey other farmers' produce and goods between the village and their markets. At first other farmers were enthusiastic but eventually they all returned to using bullock carts. They said the price they received for their produce in the market was so low that they could not afford to pay the lorry owner the price he asked for his transport services.

Case E

The Manager and the Committee had carefully studied the figures and It would be able to carry much more of the farmers' produce to the market had come to the conclusion that a truck was economically viable In the city and with its greater carrying capacity it would be much cheaper than hiring vehicles from private contractors. The Manager of the Co-operative asked the salesman if it would be possible to have the lorry delivered as soon as possible and to pay for it in 36 monthly installments. The salesman said that this was not possible. They should obtain credit from the banks or elsewhere. The Co-operative Bank was the only possible source of credit for the Co-operative but the manager could not agree to finance the purchase of the truck because of limited funds. The Co-operative had to continue to transport the farmers' produce the old way.

Case F

The Co-operative in region F bought 2 new Lorries. They were ideal for the job, but after a year the back axle of the first lorry broke and six months later the crankshaft broke on the second one. Because the Co-operative could not get replacements for these parts they transferred the back axle on the second lorry onto the first. Now the crankshaft has broken on that one, too.

Case G

The cattle farmers' Co-operative was keen to buy a lorry to carry members' cattle to the market. The Co-operative could buy a lorry with a flat-carrying surface which was big enough to carry the cattle, but it would be necessary to have sides and a roof to keep the cattle on the vehicle and protect them from the weather. It was not possible to buy a lorry properly equipped, so they decided not to buy a lorry at all.

Case H

The Co-operative was proud of its new lorry. It had automatic gears and the trouble was that drivers could never learn to use the lifting equipment properly and when any lifting equipment. It worked well at first thing broke down they usually could not mend it themselves and the Co-operative had to get somebody from the city to come and mend it. This cost a great deal of money and took a lot of time.

Case I

The local transport contractor had six vehicles. They should have been sufficient to serve the local farmers, but there always seemed to be problems. Sometimes the vehicles would arrive a day late or too early in the morning. At other times the Lorries would already be overloaded when they arrived to pick up produce. The farmers complained to the truck operator who said he would try to ensure a better service, but the same problems kept recurring.

Self-learning Activity

Try to answer the following questions on your own:

1. Discuss materials procurement and movement in cooperatives?

2. Describe internal transport and materials handling in cooperatives?
3. What do you understand from Case H under transport cases in cooperatives?

Summary

- Cooperatives practice materials management concepts in their daily routine business. They are not exceptional cases. In this chapter materials management practices in cooperatives is discussed.
- They perform procurement and movement of materials, handling, transport and other functions of materials management in their operations.

Glossary

ABC classification classification of inventory in to three groups: and a group comprising items with a large dollar volume; a B group comprising items with moderate volume and moderate dollar volume; and a group comprising items with a large volume and small dollar volume.

Base stock level the inventory level up to which stocks are replenished fixed by a periodic inventory control operating doctrine.

Bill of materials a document describing the details of an items product buildup, including all component items, her build up sequence, the quantity needed for each, and the work centers that perform the buildup sequence.

Break-even point the level of out put volume for which total costs equal total revenues.

Carrying (holding) costs costs of maintaining the inventory warehouse and protecting the inventoried items.

Delphi technique a qualitative forecasting technique in which a panel of experts working separately and not meeting arrive at a consensus through the summarizing of ideas by a skilled coordinator.

Economic order quantity (EOC) The optimal order quantity, fixed by a Q/R inventory control operating doctrine.

Flow process chart a graphic tool to analyze and categorize infestation activities so that the flow of the product throughout the overall production process is represented.

Inventory control activities that maintain stock keeping items at desired levels.

Lead time the time passing between ordering and receiving goods.

Linear programming mathematical method for selecting the optimal allocation of resources to maximize profits or minimize costs.

Materials requirements planning (MRP) a system of planning and scheduling the time phased materials requirements for production operations.

Materials management activities relating to managing the flow of materials in to and through an organization.

Open order a customer order (job) that has been launched in to production and is in process.

Periodic inventory system and operating doctrine for which record points and order quantities vary stacks are replenished up to a fixed as stock level after a field time period has passed.

Physical distribution activities relating to materials management as well as to storing and transporting finished product through the distribution system to customer.

Procurement costs of placing an order or setup costs if ordered items are manufactured by the firm.

Productivity efficiency a ratio of outputs to inputs. total factor productivity is he ratio of outputs to the total inputs of labor, capital materials and energy partial factors productivity is the ratio of outputs to one two or three of these inputs.

Purchasing activities relating to procuring materials and suppliers consumed during production.

Salvage value income from selling an asset.

Statistical forecasting models casing forward pas data in some systematic method used in time series analysis and projection.

Stockless production system a system a system of production that allows no (or as small as possible) inventors of raw materials work in process or finished goods goes hand in hand with JIT philosophy.

Work measurement the determination of the degree and quantity of labour in performing tasks.

References

Abdel-Khalik, A.R. 1985. The Effect of LIFO-switching and Firm Ownership on Executives' Pay. *Journal of Accounting Research* (Autumn): 427-447. (JSTOR link).

Aggarwal, S. C. 1985. MRP, JIT, OPT, FMS? *Harvard Business Review* (September-October): 8-10.

Agin, N. 1966. A Min-max Inventory Model. *Management Science* (March): 517-529. (JSTOR link).

Ahern, J. T. and P. L. Romano. 1979. Managing Inventories and Profits Through GMROI. *Management Accounting* (August): 22-26.

Alcide, P.E. 1986. ABCs of Inventory Management. *Practical Accountant* (August): 36.

American Management Association, Managing the Materials Functions, New York, 1959.

Ammer DS, Materials Management, Home wood, USA, 1968.

Babillus, J. 1950. Once Over Every Quarter—A Cycle Inventory. N.A.C.A. *Bulletin* (November): 274-279.

Banks, J. and R. G. Heikes. 1983. Technical Aid for EOQ Determination. *American Journal of Small Business* (Spring): 27-30.

Beaudry, D. P. Jr. 1941. The Supply Inventory and Its Control. *N.A.C.A. Bulletin* (August 1): 1381-1398.

Bomberger, E.E. 1961. Optimal Inventory Depletion Policies. *Management Science* (April): 294-303. (JSTOR link).

Cartmell, N. M. 1938. Practical Application of Inventory Control Methods. *N.A.C.A. Bulletin* (May 15): 1047-1066.

Eden, D.F. 1972. Computerized Inventory Control in a Small Company. *Management Accounting* (August): 39-42, 46.

Edwards, J.B. and D.E. Graber. 1975. LIFO: To Switch or not to Switch? *Management Accounting* (October): 35-40.

Gopal Krishnan S., Materials Management, Printice Hall, New Delhi, 2002.

Hadley, S.W. 2004. Safety Inventory Analysis: Why and how? *Strategic Finance* (September): 26-33.

Hall, T.W. 1974. Inventory Carrying Costs: A Case Study. *Management Accounting* (January): 37-39.

Lomesh S., Value Management, Oxford Publishing House, New Delhi, 1999.

Mathew P.D, Handbook of Materials Management, Calcutta 1968.

Menon K.S. Purchasing and Inventory Control, Vikas Publications, New Delhi, 2001.

Miller, A.L. 1958. Cycle counts for stores inventories. *N.A.A. Bulletin* (July): 87-91.

Mills, H.D. 1961. Inventory Valuations—An Analytic Technique. *Management Science* (October): 58-68. (JSTOR link).

Morse, D. and G. Richardson. 1983. The LIFO/FIFO Decision. *Journal of Accounting Research* (Spring): 106-127. (JSTOR link).

Murray, G. R. Jr. and E.A. Silver. 1966. A Bayesian Analysis of the Style Goods Inventory Problem. *Management Science* (July): 785-797. (JSTOR link).

Nad, L.M. 1948. Determination of 'LIFO' Inventory Valuation Under the Retail Inventory Method. N.A.C.A. Bulletin (December 15): 457-466.

Naddor, E. 1956. Some Models of Inventory and an Application. *Management Science* (July): 299-312. (JSTOR link).

Nair NK, Materials Management, Asia Publishing, 1967.

Nickerson, C.B. 1937. Inventory Valuation—The Use of Price Adjustment Accountants to Segregate Inventory Losses and Gains. *N.A.C.A. Bulletin* (October 1): 147-160.

Peckam HH, Effective Materials Management, PHI, 1972.

Philbrick, A. L. 1918. Verification of Inventories. *Journal of Accountancy* (December): 417-428.

Price, W.S. Jr. and E. J. Neppl. 1966. Automated Inventory Control. *Management Accounting* (October): 52-58.

Rhodes, J.E. 1968. Valuing Period Costs in Inventory Under Direct Costing. *Management Accounting* (February): 25-26.

Seetharaman, A. and T. D. Englebrecht. 1990. A comment on "The Effects of the Thor Power Tool decision on the LIFO/FIFO choice". *The Accounting Review* (October): 960-964. (JSTOR link).

Selden, D. W. 1960. Inventory Management—Application of the Exception Principle. *N.A.A. Bulletin* (December): 43-51. (Related to Navy Aircraft Parts).

Semier, B. H. 1952. Techniques for Control of Finished Goods Inventory. *N.A.C.A. Bulletin* (July): 1339-1346.

Severance, J. and R. R. Bottin. 1979. Work-in-process Inventory Control Through Data Base Concepts. *Management Accounting* (January): 37-41.

Taylor, J.R. 1978. Liquidation of LIFO Inventories. *Management Accounting* (April): 13-16.

Thompson, H.E. 1966. Forecasting Errors, Diversification and Inventory Fluctuations. *The Academy of Management Journal* 9(1): 67-77. (JSTOR link)

Thompson, H.E., T.L. Feder and L. J. Krajewski. 1970. Multi-item Inventory Systems with Amalgamation of Orders to Suppliers. *Decision Sciences* 1(3-4): 357-370.

Towey, J.F. 1988. Inventory Shortages. *Management Accounting* (December): 52-53.

Van DeMark, R. L. 1959. Better Inventory Classification with Less Work. *N.A.A. Bulletin* (October): 40-44.

Varma M.M., Materials Management, D & D Publishing, New Delhi, 1992.

Vich, W. F. 1925. Pricing the Inventory. *National Association of Cost Accountants Official Publications* (January 15): 3-9.

Vinson, C.E. 1972. The Cost of Ignoring Lead Time Unreliability in Inventory Theory. *Decision Sciences* 3(2): 87-105.

Weeks, T.G. 1963. A Guide to Quantity Purchasing Decisions. *N.A.A. Bulletin* (September): 43-50.

Whitin, T. M. 1954. Inventory Control Research: A Survey. *Management Science* (October): 32-40. (JSTOR link).

Whitin, T.M. 1955. Inventory Control and Price Theory. *Management Science* (October): 61-68. (JSTOR link).

Wiener, J. 1958. Controlling the 13 Elements of Work in Process. *N.A.A. Bulletin* (July): 41-55.

Zehna, P. W. 1968. A Clarification in LIFO *vs.* FIFO. *Management Science* (July): 734-735. (JSTOR link).

Zimmerman, B., D. Lefkovitz and N.S. Prywes. 1964. The Naval Aviation Supply Office Inventory Retrieval System — A Case Study in File Automation. *Management Science* (April): 421-428. (JSTOR link).

Zipkin, P. 1986. Inventory Service-level Measures: Convexity and Approximation. *Management Science* (August): 975-981.

Index

L

M

R

S

□□□